BEGGING THE QUESTION
(Roots of Deception)

By Thomas P. Lind

ISBN 978-0-9800989-1-4
      0-9800989-1-2

LIND PUBLISHING
210 Foxwood Dr. Brandon, Florida
33510-4013 Ph. 813 681 2551
mailto:tom.lind@live.com

Table of Content

A NOTE TO THE READER

Somewhere in this book I say it can be read at various levels. I know every reader will find their own, and feel the joy, and meaning behind the metaphor, simile, metonym, and the irony. Sometimes I treat a topic from a certain perspective leaving it for the reader's imagination to fill in wherever they will. For instance, the poem SEVEN BILLION PIECES, this poem should be a celebration, that we are now Seven Billion living souls on the planet. The sustenance of life in Seven Billion separate pieces of life should be an exaltation of the Human Spirit, and life itself. A miraculous accomplishment, as we know it, without precedent in the entire Cosmos.

Instead, ironically, I sing in an admonishing tone; it's like a grave ominous voice, repetitious, because I know we are barely existing; we have not transformed our vision of "Paradise on Earth" yet. In our present condition, as it is graphically written in the book, we may be headed to destruction and possible extinction. We need a paradigm shift. Why not just ask for an old-fashioned miracle? You may find it in the poems THE ABSOLUTE TRUTH or THE MYSTICAL EMBODYMENT OF LOVE. My hope is your imagination will be stirred by every topic, regardless of the angle it was written. Even so, knowledge without the proper orientation doesn't lead in the right direction. We know what to do; we just have to do it—"we just have to make the Doughnuts!"

I will give you the keys
To the Kingdom to open
The door to your inner selves,
To find self-realization,
The source of liberation.
Look with discerning eyes, an
Open mind, and open heart!

WE CANNOT AFFORD THE LUXURY

We cannot afford the luxury of wasting the mind,
On the banal, concern with the inconsequential.

Those who go hunting in a forest miss its beauty;
They are focused on the prey.

There are always unwarranted implications
In the presumption of our assumptions.

We each live and can only live at the level of our
understanding, and our perception of the world is
limited by that understanding.

From moment to moment, we are the sum total of
the thoughts and feelings we allow ourselves to
think and feel; we are only what we are
experiencing—we are our choices.

THE IMPORTANCE
OF IMAGINATION

The mind like space has no boundaries
But its imagination that fills it.

Life is a drama we live
By metaphor.

We populate the world with angels, some of us with demons, which are in turn only interpolations by a limited sensory system, of various wavelengths of energy. In days of old, we had witches and ghosts floating around, and a few dragons for good measure; now we have images in cyberspace, and aliens and a few UFO's. With as many shapes and origins as the imagination conjures.

Imagination is the medium whereby we convert an intangible, invisible world into a concrete, visible world. Where does all the esthetics, the beautiful, and the useful come from—things like music, works of art, edifices, highways and iphones? Wherever they come from—firstly, from an idea, then, imagination as the image maker, is the important step we take to bring them forth to the physical.

It was Einstein who said, "Imagination is more important than knowledge." He was ever so right, as all the assumptions we have made of ourselves, and creation is the product of our imagination. It is with imagination we invent; create mental castles in the air, and the virtual world, we live in. And it's through the recreation of mental images; we recall the patterns through which we navigate that world. The only way we recall anything is by the recreation of mental images in our minds. The only way we can state we know or feel anything is by the artifacts of a verbal and visual symbol. It matters not who we are, or where we came from, we all speak the language of imagination.

If and when, we lose these
Our world ceases to exist.
All the feelings we most cherish,
All the images we most love
Vanish, ever into the winds!

THE SPIRITUAL

It's by free will, we utter
The Name of God!
But the louder we shout, cry,
Less we are heard.

It is not my desire to preach,
But it is my sincere intent
For you to know you're spiritual,
Beyond a shadow of a doubt,
Beyond the glitter of the world!

All the beauty we all behold
Is the spiritual unfolding
In its many and varied forms.

The color of the prisms,
The harmony of various sounds—
Angels playing harps in Heaven,
To please the senses soothe the soul!

OF HEAVEN HELL

As a poet my job has always been
To create images of words
To open your minds and hearts
To let your imagination roam.

To see the beauty of waterfalls,
Hear the harmony of running brooks.
To know with imagination you make
Of hell a heaven, of heaven hell.

To know the folly of deception,
Ignorance, greed and hatred has
Deprived us of our birthright
To make the earth we live upon
Paradise!

THE GIFT OF FAITH

Faith is a gift the intellect would rob,
Never in the pilfering mind stored,
Only in the soul locked, at the bosom
Of the seas the keys, sacredly away stashed.

Never in the fickle flirting heart
For the heart overflows, skips a beat.
Faith is a gift from the infinite, only
Eternally, in the infinite to be kept.

Faith is lustrous as precious metal,
Unpolished tarnishes as metals do.
Sparkles as all fine crystal, useful too.
Uncared, shatters to a million useless pieces.

As love needs, faith too should be stroked to
endure.
Touched affectionately with care, its warmth
assures
Daily. But it's only greatly appreciated
On grievous occasion, when all has failed.

THE WIND EFFORTLESS COMPOSES POEMS.

The wind effortless composes poems.
Birds flying with every glide of their wings
thrums.
Clouds twisting and turning writes mystery plots
in prose.
Every undulation of the oceans in rhythm sings

Every wave rolling towards the shores crests in
rhyme.
Rivers peacefully murmuring put their fishes to
sleep.
Majestic oaks provide the shade for children to
play.
Snow glittering mountain peaks entice to climb.

Looking with eyes that really see even more we'll
find:
All the good and beauty of "Paradise Promised"
are here
On this planet we call earth, on this our glorious
abode!

On this wonderful magnificent mother planet, our
only home,
We can share and enjoy all the promises of the
"Promised Land".

Wishfully desiring comfort and pleasures from
Heaven won't overcome. The injustices to all
we've done!

AN AFFIRMATION OF LIFE

Within me, I carry my fountain of youth,
My river of joy, my mountain of happiness.
I drink, swim and climb beyond the limits of
My self-limitations.

Following the stars, the moon and the sun,
I go beyond the illusion of a horizon—
This is where all my days begin!

I go to sleep fulfilled, aligned with my Universe,
Contented! Grateful for the day and the night,
Grateful for the life given me!

Grateful for the love and care given
My creation—uniquely special
Among all the trillion grains of sand!

INTRODUCTION

Why do we beg the question?

To my friends, and the unbiased reader who without prejudice, fearlessly seek the truth.

Once we have been chosen, we cannot turn off that intuitive knowing that our whole life, although occasionally rocky, is an open road towards union with God. It doesn't matter the images, or the venues we take, to preserve our closeness to the divine, for we are left with a grasp beyond logic and human understanding. And in a subtle way, we become concerned, sometimes impatient, and often a little irritable, about what the world thinks. We have to be careful we don't fall into the traps of arrogance and pride. Some of us are called to live a clustered life in the service of God, others to do so in the everyday world. Whatever, we must be grateful for the providential guidance in our lives, which is nothing short of a miracle. Sometimes we feel a little out of place with the world; however, for us to live a sane life, while this is going on, we need a balanced mind and an open heart.

My mind is still active in ninety three, and although my body renegades and demands a recess, I am ignoring it. My body tries to distract me with discomforts, aches and pain, but my mind is active and alert to such tricks and draws its attention from them, and they ameliorate.

We can see how this is possible; as our latest discoveries are the mind, and the body are not two separate entities, as has traditionally thought to be by religion, philosophy and science. However, starting on the cellular level, there is intracellular, extracellular and between and among cells, a constant flow of neuronal activity and biochemical's. (The body is in constant communication with all of its parts.) These are now called "Informational Molecules and Substances." Psychosomatic doesn't have the bad connotation it used to have. A fancy euphemism, it was claimed, for some imaginary physical ailment going on only in our heads, but now we know it's a psychoneuro-physiological process going on in our entire bodies. The wisdom of the body—doesn't only reside in the "mind" but at the nucleus of every cell and neural ending, and at this level, every particle of our being is a vibrating photon. It's now a scientific understanding; the heart emits a greater field of electromagnetism than the brain. Is it any wonder, that the heart is then, just as important an organ as the brain, for knowing and feeling and seeing?

And further proof of this is the fact, the person's fortunate to have received a donated heart, after their recovery, claim to have strange and different feelings, and a new perspective of the world.

We are holographic in our nature as the Universe is, and we are unifying with the Universe and the Universe is consolidative with us. We know ourselves through the Universe, and the Universe knows itself through us. The matrix of our existence is a hologram, whereby every strand of our DNA and every star in a galaxy interacts and contains the whole and can reproduce it.

Every flight of a bird and every limb on a tree are sustained by the wind, and the inspiration of our origin is shared by every grain of sand. The ecology is in perfect balance by the constancies which keep the Universe in balance. This is why it's important we understand, each has a role to play and each life is precious. Every thought we think, every emotion we feel, as well as our deeds, must be unifying to benefit humanity; and the Universe in general.

If this was a scientific paper, I would have to be more precise in describing this, such as naming the known cell receptors, the pathways, and the neuro-peptides ligands that binds with them. And I would have to be citing the hundreds of scientific papers and research supporting these statements. However, I am writing for literate pleasure and general information. Nevertheless, in what follows I will try to bring together in a concise form the findings in the various thought discipline about our existence and our place in the Universe. First, we must keep in mind; it is getting increasingly difficult to distinguish whether scientists are writing science, or metaphysics. (Are they mystics or scientists?)

So the scientists who have the hubris to say they will find God in their laboratories are not entirely wrong. Of course, God is in the molecule, as well as in the atom and the energies whereby they are composed.   Notwithstanding, they will not be able to pulverize him in their mortars, amalgamate him in their crucibles, culture Him in their Petri dishes, see him under their microscope—and as far as the Hubble Telescope can see—He is nowhere to be found. Even so, He is everywhere all the time, and nowhere at any time. He is in their laboratories with them, if they look long enough, they will find him in their hearts.

We will talk about these things in this book, BEGGING THE QUESTION, I hope you enjoy it,

Thomas P. Lind.
Brandon, Florida,
March 26, 2013

NB

In the vernacular, when the words mystical or metaphysical are used, they seem to have an occult connotation or flavor. However, nothing can be further from the truth. First, let's deal with the word metaphysics. In philosophy, it's the branch pertaining into inquiry about an ultimate reality. Aristotle, Greek philosopher (384-322 B.C.) was first to use the word to place this thought after he had finished writing his lecture about physics. The word mystic will be much more difficult, because mystic is a subjective attitude, in contrast to occult, which is objective. What do I mean by that? The mystic is one who doesn't do anything, but by the Grace of God, the Holy Spirit infuses his being. These encounters may happen at various times throughout his life unsolicited and will change his outlook in life forever. It leaves him with a comprehension beyond logic and human understanding.   And the mystical experiences, for those who have had them, are inseparable, irreversible lasting—the understanding about the power of God in our minds and hearts leads to contentment, illumination and bliss.

Those who deal in the occult, on the other hand, deliberately set out to invoke powers from the spiritual world for their own enrichment or aggrandizement, and or, to commit malevolent acts, and have control over others. This experience leaves them frustrated and discontented—in most cases; it leaves them living a miserable life. According to this definition, we will find traces of the occult, even today, in the sense that, we see people invoking idols to intercede and bring about their desires and whims, no matter the harm it may cause to others.

Fortunately, however, we also find many groups, who are holly, dedicated people, who benefit us by their example, and have left us a rich mystical tradition. That's the discriminable difference between mysticism and occultism.

However, it must be understood, clearly; in stating this, I am not trying to defame religion in any of its forms or factions, for it is religion itself that defames religion. Through the ages and up to the present, it is radical religious factions that disrespect and war against one and other; and they denigrate and insult us and try to silence us and take away our freedom of speech and expression by coercion and violence. Even those in high authority are intimidated. All I do is call it as it is.

There is so much dishonesty going on, individually and collectively, in the world it is difficult to live a life of integrity as a genuine human being. Morality and ethical conduct have no value to a society where deception, deceit and rationalization are the norm. A society where to win is more important than justice or integrity. And this can be said to be going on at all levels, in the various significant factions of our society, such as in, law, religion, science, politics and commerce and all subsections thereof. This dishonesty is motivated and sustained by ignorance, greed and hatred.

Many great minds of the past tried to tell us that the human organism needs integrity to survive; integrity within, without and among itself, and its environment—and the tool for this is a scrupulous honesty with ourselves, and our interaction with others and the universe, and a conscientious forgiveness and gratitude. These are the three words that can save the human race. The three words that are destroying it are ignorance, greed and hatred. Honesty integrates all the facets of our being, the mental, the emotional, the physical, and the spiritual. This would place us in harmony with the spheres and in balance with the delicate constancies necessary to sustain the Universe. These are the means whereby we can live an integrated life as a genuine human being.

And the first step towards an honest world is to question ourselves. We must question every thought we have, every feeling, the attitudes we have towards certain persons, places and things. Every one of us is operating on a belief system; we have no idea how it was acquired; however, we accept it as truth, we develop it, and we hold on to it dearly unto death. Some of these beliefs are reinforced because they are considered the norm, because others believe them too, although they also do not know how, they were acquired. Nevertheless, with discretion this is not entirely bad; because we haven't developed yet to understand the mysteries of life and our existence, and if we stop to think, we shouldn't be surprised. we have to live and take our entire existence on faith.

None of us who ever lived, or anyone living today, knows the absolute truth, or what's absolutely right or absolutely wrong. I would say we must question ourselves first, then the Priest, the Scientist, the Politicians, and those in justice and law enforcement, the economic system and especially those in commerce, for all are working on the assumption that what we believe and do is correct and the absolute truth.

I am not expressing a morbid or inappropriate criticism, nor am I a fanatic cynic; all we have to do is look at the present human condition. We still have famine, incurable diseases, and wars. Inapposite deeds and deception in religion and government; corruption in law, justice, and law enforcement, as hundreds of people all over the world are arrested, and sentenced to life imprisonment and death for crimes, they have not committed. And the scientific world is just as dishonest and corrupt. It's a dog eat dog world, as there is always a mad rush to be published first and be recognized, regardless of who's discovery it is. In the commercial world, we hear daily, of people who, in one way or another, have been defrauded, swindled and robbed of his or her life savings.

At the civil and social level, every day we have murders, rapes, robberies, and accidental deaths caused by careless people. We find enjoyment in the gruesome and the ironic; otherwise, we wouldn't praise those who joke about it. We enjoy cruelty, mayhem, the macabre and the grim; otherwise, we wouldn't pay money, or stay up nights watching crime and horror movies. Do you think I am over reacting? We misguidedly call it entertainment, but I must ask, is this part of being civilized, or is it part of our ancestral traits?

It is not that the ideas behind these systems were not powerful and magnificent, but it's that all great idea's overtime loses their power through misuse, abuse, add-ones, and deletions. This is what happened to all great religions, like the ideas of Buddha, and Christ. It happens in governments too, like the ideas of Democracy and economics, and the Constitution of the United States of America. All of these now, are so contorted and distorted, they would not be recognizable by their originators.

Are you going to incarcerate me, and quiet me in solitary confinement, because I say, our whole social structure is based on deception and corruption? Are you going to crucify me too, because I am pointing out that we are not confirming to reality, and I am saying to you, it's time to lift your heads above the sand? Are you going to say I am sacrilegious, because religion, like politics, has failed us, and in many cases, they are used to exploit people? Above, I have already pointed out all the failure of society. To be complacent is to shun responsibility. However, I will have to clarify this; it's not religion or society that fails; it's the people that practice and comprise them who fail themselves.

Are you going to say I am blasphemous, because I say? We have failed to understand God? And to use all the tools he has given us, the tools of Love, Compassion, Empathy and Understanding, Forgiveness and Gratitude, Honesty and Integrity to make of earth a Paradise?   So let it be— however, I must say one more thing, it's easier to find a needle in a haystack than to find an honest person. Why do I say that, because we all must go along with the great pretension, even those in high places, otherwise we are outcasts? The best example; a politician must pretend to believe what his constituents believe, and make promises he knows he cannot fulfill; otherwise, he doesn't get their vote.

 It's a vicious circle. In all of this, I cannot stop wondering, who is fooling who? The irony here is dense like a fog; we cannot see through it. The majorities are so complacent they don't even try. As long as they are allowed to indulge themselves in a few pleasantries, and their stomachs are full they believe anything. And everyone pretends to believe what others are pretending to believe. This is an accommodation that has not allowed us to progress intellectually and spiritually; however, don't you dare to question this charade, or you will be considered a radical trouble maker. We have made a parody of life and mockery of truth. Our evolutionary development has been like a winding river flowing where there is the least resistance.

The world reflects back our attitudes, or to put it more precisely the world is a reflection of our attitudes, beliefs and our expectations. Therefore, just as ignorance begets ignorance, honesty would beget honesty—let's try it—what do we have to lose?

A Few Words About The Poem
BEGGING THE QUESTION

It seems, that life once given, assumes no responsibility for us, nor does it offer any guarantees, then the only thing that makes sense is; we must take responsibility for our lives, if we don't, we will perish at the hands of the incongruence's and injustices of life. We must be cognizant, that it is men who have the power to be just, and morality is a human affair. Nature's only concern is to balance and propagate itself. If there is a plan, or what the plan is, we never seem to know. Of course, we speculate and make assumptions.

As we look back, as far as we can through our history, we have many reasons to believe that life is an imposition. Our evolution has been slow and painful. Brutal would be a better word, because as all the other living species and organisms, we have to kill to survive. When we look at the Lion eating a Zebra, the Hyena chasing an Impala, and the Snake gorging on a Rabbit, we have to wonder how such a horrible, destructive system came about. Theologians tell us God is Omniscient, Omnipotent, and Omnipresent; meaning that he knows all things can do all things, and He is ever-present; the implications here are beyond reason. Since, it's beyond human reason to believe that an all intelligent, all powerful Being, would create such an unjust, cruel, wasteful system.

Neither religion nor science has answered these questions, which we have been asking ever since we became self-conscious beings, and are able to reflect on our condition. The answers they have given us are not factual and require a regression on top of another ad-infinitum. Take the "Big Bang" for instance; there cannot be an explosion, unless there is something to explode. And Theologians tell us in Genesis that God made a Paradise for us, but it was destroyed by disobedience. If God is Omni-potent, all powerful, how could there be any other power, besides His, that could thwart his desires and plans? To believe this, we must sidetrack our intellect and deny our power to reason. It takes the gift of Faith—unswerving, steadfast Faith!

If we are honest with ourselves, we'll find that no human that has ever lived has asked for life. In one of my poems, I wrote many years ago (1964), I said: "I did not ask for life, nor do I ask for death, why is it freely given, and so grudgingly taken back." I forgot to mention that it seems, the only privilege we have is to give meaning and purpose to our lives. This is a hard pill to swallow, but life has no meaning or purpose other than what we give it. We have to find happiness and contentment within ourselves by ourselves.

No one or anything outside of us can make us happy or contented. (I would like to mention, in passing, that contentment is a spiritual attitude. Nor are moods mere passing whims, but they have a biochemical and neurological substrata motivating and sustaining them.) And if we don't give meaning and purpose to our lives, we live in chaos, as is exemplified individually and collectively through the world by our actions.

These are compelling philosophical arguments, between which I find no solution or rest; therefore, I invariably try to assume a position of balance regarding these propositions; that life is an imposition, or that life is a privilege. I constantly say that life is as we view it, life is as we make it. What we believe is our reality, and our reality is what we believe. (Strong evidence is coming to surface now from researchers in the Neurosciences, Theatrical Physics and Quantum Mechanics that consciousness creates reality.)

I have always contended the popular belief, that there is a Universe and consciousness arise out of it, but I say that the contrary is true, there is consciousness and the Universe arises out of it; what we see and know of the Universe is purely a mental construct, based upon the limitations of the sensory system, logical reasoning, and assumptions, as far as the human intellect can take us. Moreover, however, and it's a Big But, these same researchers are opening up venues for us to more fully understand that intuitive grasp we've always had, that we are not only material beings, but we are also Spiritual. Many are saying that God is consciousness, and it is pervasive through the Universe, and it is the highest attribute of man.

Scientists are also bent on finding the ultimate principle of the Universe which at this point is called the Higg Field, and daubed by many the "God Molecule," but God will not be found in a test tube, because he is in the recesses of the human mind and heart. In light of this, we must accept that humans are complex organisms with a vast potential and yearning which never seems to be satisfied. And the reason for this could be, because we are ultimately made of energy, and energy is infinite and eternal, and in our early development, we didn't have the concept of Energy or the word Energy, we called it Spiritual. So we called ourselves spiritual and not energy beings. Therefore, our quest for a "Spiritual Life" is a valid one, if we equate spiritual with energy. Furthermore, consequently, all the confusing religions of the world will never satisfy us— because our yearnings and sense of Spirituality are more permeating and universal.

In saying God will not be found in a test tube. I am referring only to the physical aspect or the cosmology of the Universe, because the God Molecule, or the Molecule of God exists in the human organism, and the science to prove this is just around the corner, in fact, it already exists; it's purely a matter of correlating all the scattered data and formulate a theory to be scientifically validated. Perhaps what is holding us back is we haven't developed to overcome our bias to have an open mind. When in the poem BEGGING THE QUESTION, I say we must surrender, I am not saying it in a negative way, I am saying, if we surrender to something greater than we are, we become greater.

The concept we have of God differs from individual to individual, and has changed through our history. But we have to reconcile ourselves; it's the most profound, the most encompassing we've had. The most mind quelling and soul satisfying. However, we must experience it without all the flotsam, and all the debris; we have come to attach to it. Unfortunately very few have the courage to dissolve their egotistical self-concept to experience God in His pure Radiance.

When we penetrate our materiality, which also includes all our thoughts and our feelings, our preconceived ideas, we come in person with a core energy, which is self-identifying, a self originated, self-knowing and a self-directing power, and from which it seems all things originate—this is what most of us call God! It has been called by other civilizations of the past by other names, to name a few, starting no further back than with the Egyptian god Ra, which was a triad of divine father, mother and son, then to Yahweh of Israel, Brahma and Buddha of India, Allah of Islam, etc. We've had so many gods and their pantheons it would take many pages to enumerate them.

This should prove that the God experience is universal, and the human experience is not complete without it.

Now, combining our findings in the sciences and our metaphysical understanding, we can say that the ultimate wisdom is that from a pervading energy, a moving conscious principle arises culminating in the human organism, through which it manifests and knows itself. All the other complex manifestations on earth and throughout the vast, Universes must be apprehended, comprehended and understood through this conscious, moving life principle. This is why we are so right, when intuitively, we know that life is precious and must be preserved. Each of us must be grateful to be given the privilege, to consciously participate, and be an important part in this grand, magnificent scheme. And in a subtle way, we don't understand, we exert an influence on its outcome. Many of us still express concern about the dilemma of our existence; nevertheless, this is a better working hypostasis of our essential nature and underlying reality than we ever had.

In the poem BEGGING THE QUESTION, I am trying to create the imagery to help us with this transcendence, the transcendent reality in our souls. I am tempted to say closer spiritually, but

we cannot become closer to that which we are. I
have another way of saying this; we cannot pull
ourselves away from God, no matter how hard we
try, or the names we call Him:

>   He is the impulse within to move
>   Coming without shape or form,
>   Chest to heave to move the air
>   In rhyme with the atmosphere.
>
>   Beat the hearth the blood to flow,
>   Tell the cells to multiply,
>   To know, until He says no,
>   No more, the stars are fulfilled.
>
>   Jerusalem must be a citadel.
>   In the hearts and souls of men
>   Not a city in outskirts of Israel!

I do not promote any specific religion, because as
I have been saying in so many ways, the search
for God is innate, one, which never leaves us,
guiding us back to our source; furthermore, I
personally, don't identify spirituality with
religion. The spiritual man is always mindful,
calm, self-possessed and tranquil. The religious
man is always reaching for something beyond his
reach. And, to me, my sense of religion means
more than to attend a service once a week and
forget the presence of God for the other six days.
I reverence God with every breath of air I inhale
twenty-four hours a day, and I am grateful, for I
know that it's by His Grace my life is sustained.

However, this is not a judgment call on what others think and believe, as I am not prejudice towards anyone, as each of us can only live, at the level of our understanding.

However, I will leave you with a few lines quoted in John Wesley Writings, English Theologian (1703-91) by Albert C. Outler, ed., (Oxford & New York, 1964.) John Wesley was one of those who opposed the organized religion of this time. I find the following lines appropriate and more succinctly expressing my sentiments in many ways I never have:

"O Light that none can name, for it is altogether
nameless.
O Light with many names, for it is at work in all
things—
How do you mingle yourself with grass?
How, while continuing unchanged, altogether
inaccessible,
Do you preserve the nature of the grass
unconsumed?"

Remember the lines of my poem I quoted earlier, "I did not ask for life nor do I ask for death, why is it so freely given, and so grudgingly taken back?" There is a subtle sentiment expressed in these lines which seem to resonate with those expressed in that poem.

I hope all the above will be of help as you journey through life, and stop BEGGING THE

QUESTION. My hope is you'll get an awareness, which will never leave you—that we are more than the sum of our parts—basically, an impulse to form energy clusters into atoms, which form the molecules of our being. Then the cells comprising the tissues of organ systems of an organism we call ourselves. The dilemma is the individual cells of the trillion of cell composing the human body although intelligent, are not conscious, in the sense we say we are, however, when these cell's conglomerate in a collective effort to form the human organism, self-consciousness arises out of it. Wherefrom, in this process, does consciousness come from?   The Presence of God!

We must have the awareness; we are a manifestation of a power far greater than the Universe, which determines our life time and our life span. The awareness that God encompasses all things, yet he is not composed of them. He has no shape or form, beginning or end. No face to lay our hands on, but if we open our minds, he is as palpable as the beat of the heart. He is that infinite stillness always in motion at the core of our being, eternally knowing. Some way, along the way, we should take the time to be grateful.

The insight I would like to leave you with is, that we can change our world, and the world in general, if we change our assumptions, our beliefs and our expectations. .How do we do this? One thought at a time; we could only hold one thought in mind at a time. We cannot love and hate at the same time; be good and bad, benevolent and greedy at the same time. There is only one truth in the Universe, and every one of us is looking for it, some of us claim we have it, but to paraphrase St. Paul, "those who think in part, shall know in part." "For who among men knows the thoughts of a man except the man's spirit within him? In the same way, no one knows the thoughts of God except the Spirit of God." Another insight we should get is, that we should "Let go and flow free" by surrendering all those feelings and emotions blocking the free flow of our spirituality. This applies also to our physical bodies, health and happiness.

What do you think St. Paul is telling us? I think he is telling us, truth is one and simple, and it can be grasped intuitively. Not withstanding this, we set ourselves the task of gathering tons of data—we must get the facts, we say—nothing but the facts. Because of this, we have become obstinate in our opinions, bigots and a menace to our survival.

Again in my views, we don't need elaborate cathedrals for the body is the temple of God. It is not that cathedrals aren't inspiring, but with all their beauty, they are still structures of stone. We don't need multicolored vestures with gold embroidery, all we need to do is look up at the sky, see the clouds, the colors of the rainbow, and behold the magnificence of a waterfall. We don't need complex rituals, or complicated strings of words in prayer or incantations. All we need is the simple act of surrendering and let God Be— the awareness of the silence and stillness between words, as we empty our minds in meditation—it's the stillness where not the wave of a leaf stirs. It's the silence at the bottom of the oceans where not the splash of the waves is heard. It's a silence and the stillness where the synchronicity of the Absolute, the Infinity and the eternal holds.

If you must search for God outside of yourselves, you will need to find Him within yourselves first. I once said: "That if you pilgrimage to the four corners of the world to find God, if you don't carry him with you, you'll never find Him." God is not at any one place some of the times, but he is at all places all the times. We must place ourselves in a position of awareness, humility and gratitude to perceive Him, wherever we are.

> Oh, I am ever so grateful!
> Te be born destined to span
> The infinite distances of time,
> The vacuousness of space to fill,
> To know the further in space I go,
> My steps in time a soul fulfills.

Gratitude and forgiveness make us whole. Forgiveness is a two-way street, to paraphrase the Lord's Prayer: "as we beg forgiveness for our trespasses, we must forgive those who trespass against us." Gratitude is an attitude we must constantly assume, not only for the gifts and favors we have been given, regardless of the circumstances and events as they unfold in our lives, but also we must be grateful for the existence of the Universe and the privilege we have of being co-creators.

I want to share this poem with you, because I think, hopefully, it can shed some light on that intuitive longing we all have for union with, or at least some knowledge of the Devine. Unfortunately, this human spiritual experience has been smothered, and has been expressed, throughout the ages, as various conflicting beliefs and different religious practices, which ultimately become cultural institutions whose main purpose seems to be lost in time. God doesn't try to control us; he's freely given us this love, without needing anything in return. We have the freedom to love him, with the same love he gave, without expecting anything in return. To love unconditionally is the most sacred thing on earth and in heaven.

In silent prayer repeat daily:
There is no greater peace
Than a "Peace of Mind".

There is no greater comfort,
Than a child who cradles
In the arms of Eternal Love!

The watchful gaze of
A mother's love extends,
Far beyond the child!

The poem BEGGING THE QUESTION may seem strange and mysterious, but it can be read at several levels, first, for its picturesque images and pleasure of the rhythmic flow of words; second, for its mystical and metaphysical value which is revealed by deep contemplation, or meditation. In fact, the whole poem is a meditation which can attune us to our oneness with that universal, self-originated, self-knowing, self-directive creative power; we call God. To quote Shakespeare, correct me if I am wrong, I think he said: "A rose by any other name, is still a rose." I say—the same it is with God!

BEGGING THE QUESTION?

(Let "It" be risen in our hearts!)

I

When you ask me the question,
About what life really is,
It's like you asking yourself;
And answering, as if I knew,
It's as if you were lying,
As the whole world seems to do

When the Roosters crow in the morning,
There is no causality, or expectant result,
It's like the sun setting and moon rising;
Then there are the flowers nestling
In the arms of the winds.
Who questions
The Beatitude of Angels?

Why do we beg the question?

II

As I penetrate the core of my identity
I find nothing of what I thought I was.
I must resolve the "I am-ness"
Who "I" think I am,
To the nothingness it came from,
Face the God within for God is me.

The usurpation of God by the "I"
Is an aberration, for the "I" is a Delusion!

Neither "I" is God, but God is me.
He is the Being of my being,
The power that manifests and sustains me.
My consciousness is His, "I" haven't an idea how
it's made,
Every atom of my being is supported and
nurtured by Him.
Everything has its existence in this power,
Nothing without!

The obvious is superfluous
Beyond reasoning or Philosophy.

III

We must let God live in our hearts,
Then we can live in God.
When our being integrates to its wholeness,
Its Divinity and Holiness gives forth.

When the God experience becomes
The Experience of God, we see
The oneness of all things. We see
The genderless, colorless spark of Divinity
Illuminating the minds of men.

We see the self-originating pure God
Consciousness sustaining all things.
The obscuring shadows of materiality
Dissolving into the winds.

The consciousness of God is
God's consciousness becoming
Conscious of itself.
God's eternal awareness is
The infinite awareness of God
Eternally aware of itself.

God intentionally places
His attention upon his creation
Never, ever, to be withdrawn.
The inspiration of God is
Our aspiration to be Godlike.

In the Mind of God there are
No dogmas or creeds, nor does He
Theologize, only the minds of men!
We are as close to God as we
Are willing to let go
The false notions we have of Him.

The personalization of God suffers
The anguish of our prejudices and hatred.
When the personalization of God is
Transcended, beyond our bigotry,
He flows through us as what He is—
The Absolute, Infinite and Eternal!

Then the joyful blue ethereal clouds
Rise to fill the clear consciousness
Emptied of
All turbulent, confusing thoughts.
There is the illumination

Begging The Question
Of a blissful white brilliant light
As invasive as all the suns.
The sense of the individual
We very much adore dissolves
Reveling a magnificent,
Pervasive spirituality.

The ineffable visions thus experienced,
Inexpressible, too sacred to be uttered,
Are not ends in themselves,
But means to moral guidance
Through the labyrinths of earthly hell;
A means of letting go and relinquishing
Our false sense of identity to a Presence,
Unbounded, without shape or form
From which all love and compassion springs!

Surrendering, to a silence which surpasses
The harmony of all symphonies ever heard,
A solitude which encompasses the absolute,
A serenity that quells the fury of angry oceans,
A gratitude inclining the heart to worship,
An intuitive certitude
Dispelling many million doubt,
And a peace that transcends time
Healing the maladies of humanity.
And of them all—the mightiest is Love!

Why do we beg the question?

BEGGING THE QUESTION II

If there is only one God
Why do we adore so many idols?
Why do we sing hymns to a rainbow,
Ignoring the stars and the sun?

FAITH IS A GIFT

Faith is a gift from the Absolute,
with a certitude which needs no explanation.
It's living in the infinite unencumbered,
Joyfully in the eternal now.

Instead we seek peace of mind through
rationalization,
in lieu of understanding our existential position.

Of life we've made a religion, rather than find our
soul.
The android prevents us from climbing the stars.

The less we choose of the lesser evil, the less
evil we'll have; the more good we do, the better
off the planet will be.

It's a foible of human nature to celebrate the
dead, and make celebrities of an outstanding few.

We live vicariously through the prowess of
others; hero worshiping,
as though they were gods, following the herd.

The most damaging of our foibles is self-
justification, it's not conducive to good

relationships, and it's the precursor of most
mental, behavioral disease.

If we are to know our past, it would be more
accurate to know what we are doing now, than to
read history. If we are to predict the future, we
must control the present.

Of all the species on the planet, humans are the
only ones that can ask questions; by asking
questions we discover the unlimited potential of
the human mind—with the mind, we create our
existential reality, as well as all our surrealistic
fantasies.

It would be more exact to say that all history is
the intellectual history of man—the development
of awareness, consciousness, and the acquirement
of knowledge and wisdom.

Only wisdom can enlighten us; to transcend
ourselves, letting go of our self-concept to
apprehend, we are spiritual with the potential to
create our world for good or bad, heaven or hell.

Science is providing the solid foundation
For the revival in the belief in God.
It's not a revival of ritualistic fanaticism,
But of logic and reason.

IT DOESN'T SHOW IN OUR

DEMEANOR

We hate those who, the most we love,
Because we feel dependent on them.
Could this be the reason we disparage
God in so many subtle ways.
For whom should we love the most,
But our family?

Forget not, that peace in itself is power.
May the peace you seek be that of
Compassion, joy and serenity.
May the power you seek be the power
Of wisdom and love.

It would be wise to question ourselves
About all the preaching we've done?
Some claim God speaks to them,
Unfortunately, it doesn't show
In their demeanor!

A MORAL DILEMMA
WHEN IS JUSTICE DONE?

What degree of being humane can be sustained,
 Standing on shifting moral grounds? Is murder
and torture less
 Inhumane than life imprisonment? Is Capital
Punishment
More, or less inhumane than murder, torture, or
life imprisonment?

Victims of murder and torture don't have a say or
choice,
Why should the murderer and the torturer be
given one?
Is it improper to take the life of someone in
punishment?
For the murders he's done? It's true we cannot
bring back the dead,

But to spare the life of a murderer is to jeopardize
the life of many, it's said.
What empathy can we have with a killer,
If he has none?
Did the victim sympathize with the murderer
saying: I forgive
You for killing me? Did the killer say; it's not
your fault I must kill?

Wouldn't that be a cozy social arrangement?
Should we be forgiving?
Tolerate the disrespect of a human right to life,
because they say: It's
Not my fault I have this urge to kill. All our
moral issues are
A dilemma, which none of the wisest among us
has ever resolved.

The edict, an "Eye for an eye" in our scriptures is
an echo of our history.
A resounding echo of our depravity. And an echo
of a voice
In the wilderness appealing to a higher authority
to punish the Malefactors. Wasn't this the intent
of the Ten Commandments?

To set the rules of conduct, but how many of us
do follow them?
Isn't the story of the Israelites the same as ours,
corruption in the absence of law?
Law enforcement is protective and coercive; it
should be protective
Of those who are victimized, should it be
corrosive to the criminally inclined?

But must it also be punitive to be effective. The
scales of justice are swayed by
The law of retribution demanding justice is done.

Let us ponder this: Is life imprisonment less
inhumane than Capital Punishment?

Isn't it more inhumane to be imprisoned for life,
than to be put to death at once? What legal or
moral law can we invoke, other than human
rights,
To abolish Capital Punishment?

Perhaps appeal to a higher authority would be
right?
What consequences can we expect if a foreign
law is imposed on our domain?
If rifles across the boarder exported are
resounding pop, sizzle and pop,
In exchange children are snorting heroin and
cocaine, huffing and puffing
Legally, and illegal addictive drugs?

It has been proven Prohibition doesn't work!
Let the moralists answer this:
Is it inhumane to be inhumane to those who are
inhumane to us?
How about those who are inhumane to
themselves? Abusing the body, flagellating the
flesh?

Should this give us the license to invade others,
kill and torture, preemptively? Imprisoning the
minds of the young for life with antiquated
dogmas and creeds. Encroaching our mores
secretively while they sleep innocently in their
sacred homes
When is justice done?

WISDOM FROM A STONE

Expecting the ignorant to act wisely,
Is like expecting wisdom from a stone.
Nether should we expect truth from a liar.

Vipers will strike at their own shadow.
Their tongues split for one purpose
To strike from both sides of the mouth.

If we put a gun in the hands of a killer,
Isn't that the same as entrusting the care
Of your jewelry to a known thief?

If we entrust our souls to those pretending
To know the truth beyond comprehension,
Isn't that the same as entrusting our lives
To a ruthless swindler?

Expecting the ignorant to act wisely,
Is like expecting wisdom from a stone.
But a stone may have more compassion
Than those who steal our mind.

ANTI-INTELLECTUALISM

Intellects are sacrificed by emotional devotions
Logic with magic by warlocks and witches brew.
Reason dough faultless was burned at the stake.

What better ends could have preserved the earth?
What thoughts could have built a better world,
To save the human race from self-extinction?

Meaningless nonsensical hokum gurgling
Children are fed crack and pop cereal
Meaningless sounds heard rebounding through

Swollen contours of silicon breasts, spouting
Artificial milk, alluring pop culture decadence.
Balderdash, balderdash trivial resounding sounds

Jeremiads are singing lullaby hypnotic songs
Early vaccination prevents chicken pox
promoting
Cancerous politics of the uncultured growing
brain.

Weeds outgrow all the flowers we've planted
Venom from serpent's seeps if we don't stump'em
Anti-intellectualism is a disease so is anti-
rationalism.

Why don't we lift our heads above the quagmires

Of deception? Pluck the eye of anti-
intellectualism
Overcoming irrationalities by the powers of
reason?
The irony of the human situation is to know
enough
To ask questions, not enough to answer them
beyond—
The contours of the space-time continuum!

NOTE.
To this and the two previous poems: We don't have to
look too deeply to see that human behavior is mostly
illogical and irrational. Why would anyone become
adducted to tobacco, alcohol, or any other destroying
adductive drug? Why would anyone put their lives and
the lives of others in jeopardy becoming distracted,
talking and texting on a cell phone, while driving an
automobile? Why in hatred, anger, rage or self-
justification we kill? Killing, or taking the life of another,
no matter the circumstance, cannot be justified. Justifiable
Homicide is a contradiction in terms. Destroying and
killing don't relieve our hatred and anger, nor does self-
justification give us peace of mind, for it's a form of
vengefulness which eats at our souls.

Why are we hedging towards our extinction by destroying
the ecology and by all the other irrational, foolish things
we do? Could we be fulfilling a self-fulfilling prophesy?
Must life on earth be destroyed for a higher form to
evolve—the extinction of the Dinosaurs should give us
reason to be concerned? And in our wildest binge of
imagination, we have no idea what could replace us-
neither did the Dinosaurs!

WHAT HISTORY BLUR

What secrets the walls of custom hides?
Hiding what is so well hidden
The probing eyes of science cannot find,
Nor traditions dare to give a hint.

How many heads will the Emperors sword
Behead, fallen before they had time to grow?
Can spider's nets lose the trail, foul the scent
Of the hunting dogs from hell? We must save the
child!

What of the night lingering longer than it should?
Keeping the morning from rising, hiding the light
of the sun.
Where can the emotions hide our feelings
From the chilling, numbing wind, before it comes
in?

It's light that makes a difference to the searching
eye
It matters not from where it comes.
The darkness of a mother's womb seems long
Unless she aborts the child before its time to
come.

Not a chance to see the light from a candle or the
sun,

The wheels of life skidding backwards billowing
smoke
Of contraception, the sent of burning flesh is just
as bad.
Can a little coffin hide a life taken, before its time
to come?

What lines of history does history blur?
It's hard to tell what it intents to tell.
Is there a page where the light from the sun
Outlasts the darkness of the night?

The pages of history blown by the wind
Don't teach us what we should know,
Humans never learn from their errors,
Nor history keeps us from doing wrong!

History is morally devastating,
Its many pages forever revealing,
Humans have never stopped repeating
Their spiritual turpitude and follies.

History in its many million pages
Divulges many depravities and wrong
It seems we are yet to overcome.

CAN WE DIVIDE THE SOUL

Sectarians on every corner are building buildings
With dubious foundations, they call them
churches.
They fill them with different gods to confuse the
credulous.
Those of us who firmly believe only one God
made us,
Become dumbfounded; don't know to which we
should go.

These fast-food chain religion franchises are
spreading,
Popping the globe over, faster than popcorn pops
Hastily by an indifferent desert burning sun.

In many facet churches, different edition of the
Bible
We'll find, and all the verses of the gospels from
Mattlew, Mark, Luke, John, underlined
With Multicolored ink. Interpreted in various
tongues.
But the multicolored verses have one tone in
common,
The whim and the mood of those who will preach
them.

They intend to fill the hunger of human souls,But
instead, they split them, fragmentize and divide
them.
Does fast-food chain religion serve the masses?
Isn't gluttony, greed, some of our hideous sins?
Obesity of the flesh on earth can be unpleasant
and bad,
So obesity of the soul can be in the spiritual
world.

The anxiety to find the One God who made us
Comes from within the walls of the human heart,
No wall of brick and mortar can ever quell it.
If we are to worship God in a church, on an altar,
We must first find Him in our hearts to find Him
there.
We must first feed the heart with love and peace,
Forget the ignorance, bigotry, prejudice and pride
Be still; listen to the mystery of heaven with an
inner ear.
We are yet to ameliorate the spiritual hunger of
the soul!
Sectarianism neither has helped God nor man,
We are yet to know, which the right church to go
is!
A divided house is no protection from evil,
Nor can a divided soul live by inequities,
As justice is the fiber which weaves the soul.

No affront indented to the devotion
Of those who sincerely love God.
For the love of God accrues to them
Loving God with every breath inhaled!

WE LIVE CHAINED

We each live chained
To the faith of our beliefs.
We adore the trinity of gods:
Make-belief, speculation and assumption.
Never knowing the right one, nor how or why
The origins, of neither life or the Universe.
Every human lived, or about to live
Will never know how or why
Without their desire they came to be.
Why, surrendering to God's will,
Seems to be the road to peace and contentment.

Having not asked for life, we avoid death.
Hoping for answers of how and why,
We make beautiful Cathedrals
In which to kneel, and pray.
We make efficient Laboratories
In which we concoct theories without end;
With microbes and viruses we play.
We untangle the dendrites of the neuron,
Identified the biochemical transmitters,
Yet we must live, suffer and die
Never knowing why— or expecting an apology!

Never knowing why, in ignorance
We suffer the impulses of life.
Driven by greed and hatred to self-destruction,
Thinking, something went very wrong!

Hoping the soul knows the road to peace and
contentment.

Why we ask,
With all our faith,
We must kneel and cry!

My compassion stretches
Beyond the individual,
Embracing the Human Condition,
Hopefully it ennobles
All those it touches!

NOTE

Why we ask; we must kneel and cry? It's because most
humans are out of sync with each other—whereas all the
forces of the Universe are in perfect balance? They
maintain a state of equilibrium for their existence.
Humans, on the contrary, have had to decree laws, set up
law enforcement and justices all over the world;
otherwise, we would have destroyed ourselves. However,
even in the face of this we still commit atrocious crimes
daily. Neither religion nor politics have helped; neither
reward nor punishment has solved the problem. We don't
seem to have the fortitude of our convictions to control
ourselves, nor do we allow an outside force to help,
whether that force is divine or mortal. Therefore, we are
living with a moral dilemma, as well as a civil one. We
need providential intervention, badly!

THE MIND OF GOD
BEGGING THE QUESTION II

In the mirror of our consciousness/awareness
The images and sounds reflected, taken
For existence, is an illusion.

The "sense-of-self" we think we have,
The "I am" we say we are, is a delusion—
Only God can say, "I am that I am."

To paraphrase A Greek Philosopher:
The problem dear Brutus, is not
With the stars, it's we are underlings.

When we traverse the wilderness
Of imagination, we become lost
In the delusion of a Universe.

In effect we don't know who we are
And we really don't know where to go.
We grasp for straws blown by the wind,
Hoping to fill the emptiness of the soul.

We kneel and pray in devotion
Hoping to hear the whispers of a world
In a silence which has never spoken.

Begging The Question

We hope the day will come
To lift the darkness of the soul,
A light which erases the anguish of despair.
A star to guide us through the deserts,
The sands of a nowhere land

The God Mind opens a heavenly gate
Which is never broken
To roam behind the clouds barefooted,
As the angels do!

There is nothing really bad or good,
There is nothing really ugly or beautiful,
There are only degrees of the good and the
beautiful.
The higher up the scale we go, beyond our
delusions,
The closer we are to the Mind of God.

The problem Dear Brutus,
Our actions don't do justice
To our ideals!
We must open our minds
And our hearts
For the Devine light to shine
There in.

WHILE WE HAVE TIME

Even seasons when the rain downpours,
Thunders don't their roar withholds,
And lightning cracks whips of light across the
sky,
I am not stopped from building a home and
planting a tree.
Even Northwestern winds bringing gales and
storms,
These I endure and withstand.
I welcome them to feed the plants and
Quench the thirst of our dry land.

But mighty hurricane winds bringing disaster,
Blowing down the home I've built, the trees I've
planted
This I deeply helplessly deplore.

I loathe the thought of volcanoes exploding under
the seas
Rising tidal waves as high as mountains covering
The face of our mother the earth we adore.

I don't like the feel of tremors under my feet,
The cracks, gullies and the scars, the abyss
earthquakes leave,
Exposing the heart of our mother the earth we
adore.

I don't like the whirlwinds of tornadoes whisking,
Randomly scraping the ground, destruction in its
wake.
Blowing down the home I've built, trees I've
planted.

These are natural disasters called acts of God.
I will not question their purpose or intent as long
As I am spared to live and build and plant again.

But there are other disasters I deplore even more,
These are not the one's called God made, but the
one's man made:
I am scared of famine, diseases and wars—a
stranger with a knife,
Pirates of the seas, gangs writing terror with a
machine gun;
Of exploding bombs falling randomly from the
air
Leaving rings of throbbing radiation everywhere
Destroying our mother the earth we adore.

Destroying the house I've built and the trees I've
planted:
Destroying the home we call earth, and the love
of humankind,
This with resolve we should take care of, while
we have time!

WHEN IN DOUBT DO AS THE BIRDS DO

Be still, be still, my heart,
Determine where to go,
First pump blood to the brain,
Where it's needed most.

When in doubt do as the birds do,
They perch, ask the owls what they see.

The gentle breeze caressing my face
Deposit kisses of determination
On my glowing cheeks.
They are dew drops from the sky
Dripping one by one, also
                Moistures my dry and arid soul.

Puffs of affection from the heavens,
                They are too, sure?

Will the sense of "I" within survive,
The stages of life good or bad?
To float around beyond the sky.

I am not one to believe just for believing,
                To question is not to doubt
What I cannot see, much less what I do.

Neither can we prove what we see,

Nor disprove what we don't.
Does that make us somewhat agnostic?
How about Sacrilegious!

Why is it profane to search
For truth beyond the fold?
The truth which seems to be
Just beyond what we can see.

Can prayers help those who do not
pray?
Do those who do, help humanity?
How much do we have to pay for better
Results?
To question is not to weaken faith,
But to strengthen hope beyond despair.

The monuments we've made to pray,
Are monuments of determination?
Determination lifts all the angels,
Relying on what we cannot see.

Determination
Determines
Determination!

First, we must give,
For we'll only receive what we've given
When in doubt do as the birds do, they perch,
Ask the owls what they see!

If our feelings betrays us,
        What else can we do?
To transcend the infirmity
        Of moral weakness!

CONCLUSION

Why do we beg the question?

O, it was! Life would be
An open road,
Not alternate paths in a jungle hidden.
The choices we make
Straightforward steps,
Avoiding all
Our unintentional consequences!

Of all that has been said
There is always more
To be read
Between the lines.

Deception is about the most insidious state of mind we live with; it is a defense mechanism, which at sometime or another might have served a purpose. However, like our immune system, when it turns against us, it wrecks havoc. And whether we are on the giving or receiving end, we are all victims. It's insidious because it affects all of us, as the self-righteous and honest also displays traces of it. It is an armour our; we use to protect the frailty of our egos. And we feel we must always be on the defense to hide our inner thoughts and feelings from the praying minds of others; and, we also make good use of it to exert control over others.

We are born in ignorance, and it is hard to grow out of it; and deception, greed and hatred are the traits we developed in our early days when we were scavenging through the jungles for survival. We have also learned through trial and error that we have other powers, such as love, gratitude, forgiveness and compassion. The problem, it's taking a longtime to learn how to use, these tools to benefit the human race. We have not learned that we can love unconditionally, that we can carry an attitude of gratefulness and forgiveness in our minds; and develop sympathy, understanding and compassion for others—and others can do the same for us.

Let us all come together to the realization that we have the tools to make the world a better place. With love, gratitude, forgiveness and compassion, we can uproot deception, ignorance, greed and hatred. And make of earth a Paradise.

One of our major problems is that we have been living in a Manichaean, fragmented world by adhering to a dualistic philosophy, which states the Universe is always reducible to two distinct parts. René Descartes (1596-1650) French philosopher, who was considered a great philosopher of his time, and even so, now, by many—carried this idea further to please the authority of the church by postulating the body and the soul were two separate entities, which didn't affect each other, any interaction between them, would need the intervention of God. This philosophical view has had an extreme influence in our lives, and has prevailed through all our disciplines of thought. It has been a detriment to our development, until now.

Today Scientists are concerned with a unified theory of the Universe, and the discoveries in Quantum Mechanics. And serious research in the human sciences has proven; a human is whole, body, mind, and emotions; and they know these don't work separately, or independently, but they function dependently as a whole integrated system. Traditionally, because we believe in a dualistic philosophy, we thought that our physical body, our mental body, our emotional body, and our spiritual bodies were separate, and work independently of one another, but now we know they don't.

Every problem has within itself the answer; it's like a mathematical equation, and all we have to do, see the relationship between its parts to discover the answer. The problem is, most of us don't see it, either we don't take the time to do so, or we don't have the capacity. There is a cognitive dissonance which blocks our understanding. Each of us can only live at the level of our understanding, and our perceptions are limited by that understanding.

We may be correct in assuming we share a common world. But each of us is doing so limited by the particular frames of our sensory faculties, and our intellectual insightfulness, strengthened by the wiring of our brains; and the beliefs we have internalized. That's why we have so many conflicting world views and what our existence is. The redundancy of the questions we ask entraps us as a squirrel in a cage, but we don't know we are trapped, because we are revolving with the cage. God exists, because he exists. Why existence exists? Because it exists, otherwise we would not be asking the question.

At the beginning, I promised you to know, you're spiritual, beyond a shadow of a doubt, beyond the glitter of the world. I am presenting a strong argument for such a position. I am aware some will dispute it, but I feel that reason will prevail. Its common knowledge now, the Universe is an expression of an infinite and eternal energy, which seems never to lessen. And although this energy is invisible, we know it exist, and we know scientifically that energy is converted to matter, and matter is converted to energy. These various conglomerations of matter of different sizes are affected and influenced by an invisible force, which exerts power over, though, and on them. This force is called the gravitational force, and it is a form of energy. And since we can equate energy with spiritual, we can say the Universe is spiritual.

A human, is comprised physically of the same elemental particles, which comprises the Universe, in other words; we find the same elements in the human body as are in the Universe—atom for atom, a molecule for molecule. And for all practical purpose, they are the same. They are the same, except for one exception, which is, that humans are self-conscious. This self-consciousness is an invisible energy, from which an invisible function we call the mind manifests. The power of this invisible mind is to bring forth ideas from an invisible world, expressed in audible sounds and visible images. And again, since an invisible energy being forth all this we can equate with spiritual, we can say all humans are spiritual.

Here are a few ideas and words to play with, about our redundancy, and how we are always begging the question. If we ask someone, if he has stopped lying, whether he answers no, yes, or when, it would imply he has been lying. When we ask if something is right or wrong, whether we answer in the affirmative or negative about either question, we are implying an answer to the other. We use the word, The Absolute, as a synonym for God, and whichever word we use, carries the seed of the concepts of Infinity and Eternity. And if we use the words infinity and eternity, we are implying they are absolute, and that all three are qualities of God.

To be aware of awareness is to be aware of existence, beyond cause and effect—because reality is simultaneous, without cause or effect, with the point of observation. At that point, is where all the forces, which bring the Universe into existence, conglomerates—as consciousness, movement and being. That is where God is. Wherever this focal point of observation moves, the universe moves, and from wherever we observe the Universe, the Universe sees us. And as the Universe sees us, God sees us, and we see God.

Whatever dimensions we project to the Universe; the Universe reflects to us. We are not the cause or the effect of the universe because we are simultaneous with it. At the point of awareness is where we come into existence as well as the Universe. And the greatest power humans have is the power of intent; with the power of intent we can direct, consciously or subconsciously, the minutest impulse of our mind, and we change our DNA, our biology as well as the face of the earth.

Our thoughts may originate from the firings of neurotransmitters, and our emotions may have biochemical underpinnings, but ultimately they are energy and spiritual. Is it any wonder then why many scientists turn to a spiritual life? At the bottom of everything, we are left with this incompressible field of visible and invisible energy, which is self originated, self-perpetuating and self-knowing.

Our reality is what we believe, and what we believe is our reality. The human brain has this enormous ability to make maps. To categorize, classify, make designs, and points of reference which it files in folders of memory—it projects these to an undefined, unformed field, we name energy, this is reflected to us as the universe. And with the language of mathematics, our projections are made more credible, and to a certain extent more beneficial.

Life originates from this vast "Field" of energy, with the power of conscious/awareness to behold itself. Reason would lead us to believe this is not unique to planet earth. However, wherever it manifests it would be unreasonable not to believe life could be different in atomic, molecular and physical structure and intellectual capacity from all living specie on planet earth. The universe as we know it is a creation of the human mind. The Absolute, the Infinite, the Eternal are supreme points of reference; we have created to navigate our Universe.

They are our bench-marks to transcend ourselves—the eventual objective of evolution and our existence is—self-transcendence—from the single cell to the multiple, to the primate, to God.

As I said at the beginning: Life is a drama we live; by metaphor.

Each life form is an expression
Of its own existence.
Existence in itself is not a state,
But a state of conscious/awareness.

The Universe as we know it
Is a projection of the human mind,
And even amongst us,
We each experience it differently.

It matters not
The black holes we discover
The million galaxies we find,
It's all a view of the human mind.

The Human brain and the Universe intertwines,
More so than the spiraling galaxies.
The evolution of the Universe is
As much as, the evolution of the brain.
A self-perpetuating reciprocity without end.

Don't give up hope just yet,
Right around the corner,
You my find, the right road to take.

It's gratifying to know,
It could boil down to
A joyous, happy, state of mind.

The sway of a rose is a poem
By the wind.

Begging The Question

The frolicking ants across a hill
A Royal Ballet.
Works of art the rays of the sun.
Every line of a pen, the swing of a baton,
Every touch of the toes on the ground
A dance—an eternal skill!
The harmony of life every choir sings.
From the first to the last breath—a symphony!

THE LEAVES OF AUTUMN

The autumn of our life with
All the multicolored leaves sparkling
Is a time for repose! Each leaf a
Memory of the storms withstood,
And all kisses the winds blew.

When in the fall the leaves all turn
Yellow and red and the golden
Brown ones blown on the waiting ground
Covering the weeds, which had grown,
It's to remember spring, that's been!

It is time to give thanks for the summers,
The sunshine and shade, the rain and the wind,
Graciously foretelling peace of *fall* to come;
Thanks to the gardener whose hands planted
seeds,
Beautiful trees, shrubs the snows overcome.

The deeds of our lives much like the leaves
Of fall, color and shelter the sorrows,
And brings joy to our accomplishments:
Roses in the garden, children's laughter,
Poetry read—O, the autumn of life!

A time to remember all our joys,
A time to give thanks for what was planted

Generously the whole world to delight.
Seasons come and go, prayers answering
In winter, spring, summer and in the *fall*!

The best season of our life is fall,
When time with pleasure is right, orange ripe,
Harvesting all the fruits we have planted!
Remembering all the lives we have touched,
The tears we shared, the songs we've heard!

SEVEN BILLION PIECES

Seven billion pieces of rags to wipe
  The sun for it to shine again,
Seven billion synapses to snap for
  The brain to think a thought again,

Seven billion pieces of broken lives
  To mend for souls to be again.
Seven billion human bodies will be dead
  If we don't mend all the harm done,

To this the one and only world we have,
  To this the one life we've destroyed!
Seven billion pieces of human thought
  To mend to live a life of joy again!

YES HE CAN

It's the dare to question,
Makes us heroes.

What other object can a human have?
But to know as much as, he possibly can,
To be as much as he can possibly be.

His capacity to rise above his level
Of understanding is beyond
The boundaries of space, the limits of time.

If he wants to roam the heavens with angels,
He can. If he aspires to be godlike he can.

He has already conquered the jungles
And swamps,
He must now conquer his mind
To traverse the wormholes of space.

What lies beyond, only he can,
Ever know,
Only he can expand his level
Of understanding!

AS THE SAINTS DO

When we awoke to this world,
We expected to find
All the comforts we had in heaven.

We didn't know how harsh
It would be,
Yet we preserved and preserved,

With cleaving claws to cling
To find joy in the life us given.
We crawled, we stood and we climbed,
As we each still does,
Hoping to find the way back to eternity.

This conscious dweller,
Who dwelled within the clouds,
Now within walls of flesh confined.

Grieves as all mortals do,
Forever seeking to be free
From the imprisoning images
Of the alluring senses.

To regain its wings of liberty
And be free forevermore;

To roam the heavens as its brethren,
The Saints do.

Epilogue

THE BEGGING OF THE QUESTION
IS A COP-OUT

My dear fellow humans, there is nothing random or chaotic about the Universe; and as William James, great American Psychologist, once said— "If we move one grain of sand, we disturb the equilibrium of the Universe."

I say, a thought can change the Universe; evidence, we have changed the planet with our thoughts. We have changed the flow of mighty rivers, built bridges over swamps, and cities where elephants would have roamed.

It's the human mind, which creates the magnificent, the beautiful, the true and the good; as well as, the ugly, the evil, the erotic and the erratic; and of these, we make the world we live in.

However, we shouldn't let any impulse, sensation, or feelings decide what our life will be. They have no meaning or purpose until we give them one by naming them, jealousy, hatred, anger or rage. Otherwise, that's all they are, purposeless nervous twitches without a name. And all the various sentiments without the proper intent could be just as bad. If you want to direct our life to happiness and contentment, then we must control our impulses of intent and clothe them with beautiful positive words, Love, Compassion, Empathy, Understanding and Joy. We have to remember, any thought or emotion we are experiencing, reverberates through our entire bodies down to the molecular; and who know, it may shake-up the atoms too, as well as the Universe.

Our greatest task is to understand and control the mind; learn to think with honesty, genuineness, integrity, gratitude, and forgiveness—and above all give unconditional love—isn't this how we envision it to be, in Heaven?

It is said, we are creatures of habit and ritual, users of symbols living by metaphor and with this, I wholeheartedly agree. Once a thought or an act is repeatedly preformed it became ingrained as a neural pattern which is relegated to the automatic nervous system for machinelike responding; it then became difficult to reverse. It needs no conscious effort, intent or reason, to perpetuate itself. We become puppet's or better still zombies, dancing without music. We are the victims of our habits—our habits of thought, beliefs, feelings and behavior. And since, we create these, we can control them.

This is also, how rituals come about; when a ritual is performed routinely, thoughtlessly, it becomes a habit, and it looses its meaning and purpose, and the spark of its originality and joy. It's like dancing without music, the night without a moon, the day without the sum. It's like dead love pretending to love. Rituals are also addictive, as any of the mind and mood-altering substances; we thoughtlessly acquire the habit to use.

And as far as symbols and metaphors, since we don't know what reality is, we symbolize it, and every thought we think is a metaphor. We assume that to have some touch with reality; we must rationalize life, but a rationalization is a symbolization of something we think is, the way we think it is.

Is it any wonder, we find it difficult to come to a consensus, about what our existence is, and how we should live our lives?

Anything, of which we do not know the immediate cause, is a mystery to us; and when we assume a cause without a cause, it becomes more mysterious. The conception we have of God is one of the such mysteries. Our sense of reason tells us there must be a cause for everything, but our sense of logic refutes some of the assumption we make. Therefore, we are left with the dilemma, that, because of limits of the intellect, we cannot know the origins of our existence, and we find it hard to believe, the things we cannot see or touch, logically reason out to a palpable conclusion.   So we cannot believe there is a principle which is the cause of all things.

Thomas Aquinas, Italian Theologian (1225-1274), tells us God is the uncaused, cause of all things. Humans in general are constantly in a state of a free floating existential anxiety, and are incessantly seeking mental closure and emotional balance, because they feel disconnected from some indefinable source. However, no matter the condition we are in, either of poverty or wealth, sickness or health, nothing seems to provide the closure and balance we are seeking, but a connection to, and a belief in a power, which created and protected us, a power far greater than anything we can conceive in the Universe; we call God. It seems Saint Aquinas had an insight; we are just beginning to grasp.

THE MAGNIFICENT GRAIN OF SAND

True love is spontaneous,
Continues,
It does not stop or start
With every skip of the heart!

We are yet to find
The sparkle which lights
The fires of love.

The Exploder of the "Big Bang"
The active principle as the prime cause
Of the explosion!

The precision for the inception
And the continuance of life is
Within a nanosecond of time,
Within the space of an atom,
A Planck's magnitude of a particle,
And much further beyond.

To whom should we be grateful
For the precision which sustains life,
And the Universe,
For its continuance and subsistence?

For The magnificent grain of sand,
On which without complaining,
We've been given the privilege
To sleep, to live and stand.

For a sparkling droplet of water,
A caressing puff of wind,
The shining moon, the rolling
Clouds, the colors of a sunset?

A DIFFERENT GRAIN OF SAND.

Of all the laudatory praises I sing
One is to me,

For with all my deception
Lies and frustrations, I am
A different grain of sand.

One in his image and likeness
A creator has made.

If at times, I seem
Dumb and confounded,
It's because my body weighs more;
It keeps my heart earthbound entrapped,
As well as my ethereal soul!

For some confounding reason
With all my failures,
I haven't lost my vision of Heaven!

It's the faith I carry to sleep,
Awakes me in the morning!

APPENDIX
Our Existential Nature

A further clarification of our existential nature: There is a vast sea of consciousness and movement within us, which corresponds with what we perceive without, and both the consciousness and the movement, within and without are simultaneous with each other. It's a constant knowing and doing, which are instantaneous with each other, but unless we intentionally put our attention upon it, it eludes, and it seems there is a loss of awareness. In other words, it's through this simultaneous flow to move and to know we become.

From this vast potential sea of consciousness and movement, intentionally or unintentionally our thoughts and imagination arise.   And we are influenced and become whichever of these we entertain. Then we are dominated by those with which we identify and become attached.

Our basic existential position is to know and to do, and by this we become. and pursue the ideal we envision. Therefore, we become whatever we think, and we do. However, our existential nature remains unimpressed, unaffected, neutral, and we have choice and alternatives. Consequently, we really need not be affected by our thoughts and actions, unless we let them. If we become complacent and don't act intentionally upon the world, the world will entrench its whims upon us.

Acting intentionally on the world, means more precisely, our actions should exert a positive, constructive influence on life; and we should be participants, in the spiral evolutionary development of life—we take life for granted, not realizing how precious it is—life is delicate, and is just as enigmatic a mystery as the origins of The Universe.

For emphasis, I will repeat myself: The maladies of the human race are the cancerous cells of ignorance, greed and hatred, and they mitotically divide through the entire body spreading deception, pretension and rationalization; and the most honest and sincere of those among us, no matter how subtle, are affected by it. We live in a state of pretension and make-belief, which outwits the fairytales of Alice in Wonderland— always in the shadows of the realism of our existential reality.

Nevertheless, we can cure ourselves by crawling out of the Rabbit hole aboveground, to see the sunshine and inhale a fresh breath of air. Seek understanding; living wisely, benevolently and compassionately by the altruism of our creative minds. As I've said before, imagination is the magic carpet, by which we can soar beyond the heavens. Use it to create a world of joy and contentment; based on the acceptance of our existential position, not on rationalization, deception and lies. This is the one issue of our existence; I am fanatic about, and the motivating drive of my intent, is no other, but for us to see through the deception.

There is also something more, I would like to emphasize. I have been admonishing that we should empathize and develop empathy towards others, but empathy is more than trying to understand another. It's entering into the feelings of others and their state of mind, and has a spiritual and therapeutic value. We must be aware that our senses are extracorporeal, and extends far beyond any imaginary border, merging and mingling with the senses of others through the medium of space. We may say, this is a far-out idea, but it is not, when we consider all the science involved. First, we know that our world is an interpretation of various wavelengths of the electromagnet field, by our senses.

Then, remember that space, according to Einstein's theories, is not empty or a vacuum but substantial with its own characteristics and mysteries, which sustains the expanding Universe—therefore, the interconnectedness of all things. This also means that all humans are interconnected not only by their senses, but by the mind, the electromagnet field, gravity, and all other substances that constitute space. Therefore, we can say that empathy is spiritual, a deeper interconnectedness we have with others—as well as with the Universe.

However, we must proceed with caution: Because we say, everything is interconnected to everything in the Universe, that doesn't mean anything is necessary, or that something is the cause of something else. The evolutionary process allows for inter- origination in a derivative sequence, but that doesn't mean something is the prime cause of something else. Only God can be said to be the necessary cause of all things. Furthermore, it doesn't mean anything has an essential nature, or is unfolding towards an ideal.

Neither God nor evolution can be said to have an end in view, for that would be falling through the traps of the Essentialist, the Creationist and Determinism. That would deny God's greatest gifts to man— Free Will and Love.

What we are saying here shouldn't be taken as a contradiction of what was said in the opening paragraph of the Epilogue. For the constancies required to make the Universe and life possible, and keep the planets in their orbits is maintained by the balance of mass and gravity.

The most outstanding features of the Universe and life are movement, change, balance and consciousness. For human's, balance translated to harmony among all things; movement, change and consciousness, to know, to do, and to be. And love encompasses all.

Consciousness is the creator of reality as we knew it. What reality is outside the consciousness box, we cannot know, nor will we ever come to know. We have the potential to expand our knowledge to the limits of consciousness, and as we do so, our existence takes on other dimensions, but although consciousness is boundless, our knowledge always seems to stop near the edge of an unknown frontier, which for all practical purposes appear unattainable.

However, we must not lose sight of the fact; we have the power to expand our knowledge. Without the potential to know more, love more, and be more, existence would be limited, and life would be boring. It would not be worthwhile living. Fortunately, for us, life dangles many Carrots in front of us, and the pursuit is its own reward. Self-consciousness gives us the ability to question ourselves and our existence creating the human dilemma; a predicament that has evaded the greatest mind from antiquity, and will challenge all the intellects yet to come.

Optimistically, we may come to know how we came into existence, by studying the physical laws of the Universe, but we will not know for what or why. Our sense of identity, which never leaves us until we die (only if the brain becomes diseased), needs consciousness/awareness to float around in—without consciousness and self-consciousness our sense of self would be lost, and we wouldn't know we exist. And neither would the Universe.

Scientists are telling us they are on the verge of discovering how our sense of identity is formed—our sense of self, which when as a child, unaware of its development, suddenly it dawns on us; we are a self-aware being. Once we are self-conscious, we are attuned to the universal consciousness field which brings the Universe into existence, and sustains it. I have said this before, elsewhere, that consciousness is a force field, just as important as gravity, perhaps even more so.

We must hold judgment, as to whether scientists will discover the origins of self-consciousness and consciousness, until further developments; at this point, it seems the approach they are taking is on the wrong track. It does not go beyond the capacity of the brain to acquire knowledge and memory; which to me are secondary and not primary causes. Perhaps as they go along, they will formulate a more viable hypothesis.

This reminds me of the Chicken and Egg problem—which came first? Applying this to the brain, we ask. Did the brain come first, and then consciousness arose out of it? Or is it conscious, aware intelligence that exists first, and then creates the brain through which it expresses itself? Isn't it more plausible to believe that conscious, aware intelligence came first?

This doesn't refute evolution; on the contrary, we can see how evolution is necessary to a principle which needs to create a medium through which to express it. And the medium it creates has to be reflective, as the human brain is, for it to know itself.

Another dilemma is the concept of the Absolute; many Philosophers have said that there is no absolute in the universe, which would mean that there is no Absolute Creator. I would say that the absolute is absolute unto itself; however, in the created world, there are on absolutes. And in an expanding infinity Universe, the first order is movement and change. Paradoxically, we give more prominence to our illusory perception of permanency and stability than to change. We perceive movement vividly and we love it, but relegate change to an unperceivable background. And just as we don't perceive the Universe expanding, we don't perceive man has the seeds of his redemption within himself. History has had its virtuous who understands this, but we rarely emulate them.

Furthermore, the concept of the Absolute has implications, which can be confusing. It has been used in a different sense in mathematics, politics, theology, and philosophy. Here we are not concerned with mathematics, which speaks of carrying numbers and circulations to their absolute and infinite power, nor are we concerned with political science that states Kings, and governments have an absolute right to rule over its citizens, with or without the assumption, of "supreme perpetual power." Neither are we concerned with theology, whose assumptions are the same. However, we are concerned in the philosophical sense where the concept implies absolute perfection, and fullness. Even though, our experience tells us nothing in the Universe is perfect, nor in any sense of the word, the Universe is full. And we also have a conflict with infinity and eternity as they imply absolutes.

It's by intuition; we grasp abstract concepts. The descriptive terms applied to them, vaguely hint at their meaning, or magnitude. Intuition also gives us a certitude no explanatory descriptive term can, about many of the mysteries of the Universe.

Nevertheless, nothing is ever lost, and as we are Co-creators, through the power of hybridization, we have transformed many species of plant and animal life to satiate our hunger and delight our senses. Engorge our intellects with infinite possibilities. Many of our art forms are sculpture in stone, words to poetry, colors to dimensions in space, and sounds to music. However, our greatest accomplishment is to turn art to science to sculpture new life forms from a pool of genes. Fortunately only God knows the limits to our possibilities, may they turn out for the greater good.

IT'S BETTER TO LAUGH.

The joke could very well
Be on us.
Who betrays us
But ourselves.

Like so many things in life,
Humor is ironic.
Why is it an occasion of mirth,
To see someone slip
On a Banana peel?
Why is it amusing to see
A Monkey holding up
An umbrella while he is
Imitating what he sees?

It's somewhat ironic,
We don't know who
Is mimicking who?
It could be, all the irony,
The laughter is a big joke
A Jester is playing on us!

Isn't it a whole lot better given
The choice, to laugh, than to cry!
We've heard it said—
Laughter is therapeutic!

When we take ourselves seriously,
We become philosophically morbid.

When we laugh, we make merriment
To dance through life! Of Jesters
We should make Kings! God must have
A sense of humor,
How else He tolerates us!
His perhaps is the loudest laugh!

However, this book should not be taken lightly, because it is a book of therapy and solace for what ails the Human Race. Man has become alienated from himself, his fellowmen, and the Universe—from the idea that neither life nor the Universe is random or spontaneous; and that it+ is by the Grace of God; man is, the interconnecting link of all things. Read it several times with this in mind.

The atoms of our emotions
And the molecules of our thoughts
Reverberate with the waves
Of the electromagnet field.
They resonate with our empathy
Influencing all
Within its range of motion.
The blossoming of which is
Love and understanding!

WHO AM I?

The "I" which thought itself to be
Other than it is, once released,
Vanished like a cloud beyond the sky.
Then it has no shape or form,
No color, prejudices or creed.

It is smaller than an atom, yet
Taller than the highest mountain.
It is in itself what it has always been,
The energy from which all springs.

Once the ego is exposed, for what it is
It flees of its own accord. The sense
Of self, which thought itself to
Dominate the world vanishes
With every new cloud.

Once the gate is open
The threshold crossed,
Seen the beauty of the other world,
Who would foolishly return?

We've vehemently discussed this subject in the poem A Moral Dilemma, When is Justice Done? However, it's such an important issue, it must be repeated many times, perhaps its message will be heard, and make an impact on our future behavior.

WHY WE DESTROY

When you pull the trigger of a gun,
Pointing to someone before you,
Or to others randomly, it's humans
Like yourself you have destroyed.

You should stop and ask yourself:
What gives me the right to kill?

Precisely and literally speaking
We don't own our bodies,
Much less the body of others.
How dare we destroy it?

You didn't bring yourself to life,
Some complex higher power did.
You have no right to destruct
What you have not made!

When we violate another's life,
We annihilate the nobleness
Of the human spirit. Senselessly
We've clipped an angel's wing.

To esteem life is to reverence
Our existence with passion,
Embrace the oneness of our being
With the Universe in mutual love.

THE SOUL IS ONE

Science is direly trying to discover,
What the words of the Poet reveals.

The soul is the soul of God.
The light of the sun sustains
The balance for life to bloom.

The soul is but one
From which like a sparkle of the sum
All souls emanate,
Each with its own individuality,
And a personality of their own.

The sum has its life of its own
And effervesces life around
The globe to be born
In many forms again and again.
The soul and the sun shines
In multiple directions,
As indiscrete as consciousness is.

And as a hologram all is one,
From the one soul other souls
Are born, and like a mother's arms
They unfurl and enfold their own,
And gather them back in the womb,
When the time has come.

A PRAYER FOR THE INCLINED

Thank you God
For all my sorrows and joys
For that has made me
What I am.

I accept my life unconditionally
The way it unfolds.

Many times I have lost the road
I should have traveled,
But your guidance never fails.

I am grateful for all your gifts,
For your tolerance and understanding
Of my failures, my pretentions,
And the million chances to redeem.

My gratitude exceeds far beyond
Any disappointment or expectation.
Thy Will, be done!

WITH OUT THE EMOTIONS
THE SPIRT DIES

Neither Love nor God can be rationalized; Theologians and Philosophers have been trying to do so, unsuccessfully, for ages. When we intellectualize them, they get lost in jungles of thoughts. Only by the emotions they fill our hearts. Words in themselves are merely symbols, without a trace of feelings. At times, they can also be deceiving, when we take them as signs; they may point to something, which isn't there.

It's with the emotions; we savor the many flavors and the mysteries of life. I am not minimizing the importance of logic or the intellect, nor throwing reason out the window, but only emphasizing the important roll the emotions play in our lives. Therefore, this is written with passion and love, and because of the love of God—fortunately, God always reciprocates more with love than with reason.

HONESTY

Unfortunate but pertinent, the most astute, shrewd and calculating of those among us to the village idiot, what they know is what they think they know, and nothing more; and they are only living at the level of their understanding. Anything other than that is self-deception, pretension, or a deliberate intent to deceive.

What I am saying, and what I've said, is not said with arrogance, nor is it a matter of pride.

I've said enough about this. However, Humans left to themselves and by themselves, have little to be proud about, up to this point in their history. It's only when they relied on a higher power, they made sense. This is an existential fact. Nevertheless, that's what I think I know and feel sincerely, humbled, unpretentious, at this level of my understanding.

This, I don't think is an unusual or irrational stance to take, by anyone seeking the truth. We should fervidly pray for guidance to stop blaming others and the world, and take responsibility for our actions and reactions, our inadequateness and our beliefs. Think of this, the simple act of being honest and responsible can change the world.

BEGGING THE QUESTION III

Turn the night to day
Let not arrogance stand in the way
Of our reality, for whatever it is,
Our Reality is only an interpretation,
Of the phenomenal, human brain.
The minds of the young brain
To perceive without predilection,
Without prejudice, dogmas or creeds—
Create a better reality than we've created!

WHY WE BEG THE QUESTION

We must blame our disappointments on our expectations, not the world! But, neither should we blame ourselves for lost opportunities, if we didn't have them.

This of course, does leave us begging the question; the   perennial question of how and why we came to be, which in the first place, we are not smart enough to answer, nor have we the slightest clue, if there is an answer, we can comprehend.

Many, however, consider him who surrenders, without a try, a coward. But then it's the brave who dies not the coward. The incongruity!

Success is what we achieve by intention, failure happens by attrition,
Neither can we receive from anyone, nor give anyone, that which we do not have.

If someone promises more than they have, this not altruism, but stupidity.
We become gullible, wanting badly to believe, and are deceived, by those themselves deceived.

Some of us are victims not by choice, but the
majorities of us are; we victimize ourselves.
Not all martyrs will be considered for sainthood,
nor dying for the wrong cause make us heroes.
Valor is the drive to survive, surmount all the
battles of life.

We get out of life only what we put into it,
sometimes less, never more.
However, we must know what we want to get it.
Apparently, seemingly the world is not fair: And
there are no guarantees.

The rich by their endeavors seem to have more
than they can use. Not the poor who need it. The
poor
Never knowing what they want, never get it.

Irony! Wealth is not something tangible; it's an
Assumed value, exchanged for things we don't
produce. However, if we consume all the soil,
drink all the water; pollute the air, the story ends.
We will not survive!

Other dishonorable things we should mention:
The Armor the ego wears is Pretension,
Rationalization the mask communally we share
with all, not only on auspicious occasions!

The ego adulates itself in Hero Worshiping,
aggrandizes in the Herd Mentality. Indolently, we
bask in the shadows of achievement of others.

By the strength of our beliefs, we develop our faith, but it is by our faith, we hold on to our beliefs, whether right or wrong!

THE IDOLS WE ADORE

We cannot see the delusion
We're part off, partaking in,
Nor the blind his hand
Groping in the dark:

Whatever our assumptions,
But leads to the conclusion,
We predicate of them.

Oh! The magic of the mind!

Assuming answers predestined,
We beg the question by
Our circular thinking.

The idols we adore
Are not worthy the worship,
We place on them,

Neither falsehood turned truth
Reveals a destiny foretold,
Nor can we transform
Fantasies to reality.

Why we waste time
Worshipping nonexistent things?

Wishfully thinking they're,
More than:

The magic of the mind!

Oh! The idols we adore!
No one can sell us,
What he has no right to sell?
Or, rewards free passage to heaven!

WHO IS THE ONE PERCEIVING

I don't intent to be ambiguous,
But our reality is lost in none existing time.
I cannot see traces of my origin
Before outbursts of the "Big Bang".
Nor can I behold the magic wand
Of dogmatic, deterministic gods.
All around we can see stars emerging
Flying away in undetermined space.
The coherence and correlation of my senses
Can sense beyond various streaks,
But who is it, the one perceiving?
Is my identity subservient to my subconscious?
Or lost in consciousness whims.
The mysteries of our realization
Staggers and strains the imagination!
I don't intent to be ambivalent,
Nor confusing,
By the reaches of the mind's eye!

IT HASEN'T LEARNED TO HATE YET

A child is born!
From a new roll a carpet spreads
Waiting for little steps.
Crawling, pushing up,
They haven't learned to walk,
As yet.

A room painted, blue or red
A crib decorates the center
With squeaky, shiny toys overhead.
All items of endearment!
Benignancy of expectant parents.

A bawl is heard through corridors,
From the new born.
Not a cry, it hasn't learned to cry,
As yet.
It yearns for attention,
Is hasn't learned about love
As yet.

Not binding with the plastic
Bottle given to suckle.
With lips open, craves,
It prefers the warm nipples

Of a mother's breast,
Sensing the warmth of her flesh,
Hungers her hug it learns to love.

It hasn't opened its eyes yet
Doesn't know there is a world outside
Waiting,
It hasn't learned about hate,
As yet.
Tomorrow eyes will open,
And learn to hate! To love!
Learn to speak dirty words,
Perhaps to Pray?

A Sestina

THE SECRET OF LIFE

If the heavens were to open its gates revealing its
hidden wisdom,
Can we come to understand the many mysteries
of life?
Would we come to know the importance of
giving to receive love?
Can the confabulation be stopped helping the
deceived?
How many can we bring to the fulfillment of the
dream of heaven?
Guiding children by hand to the achievement of
their aspirations.

Will men forever be degrading one another
denying their aspirations?
Contriving to turn all knowledge into evil, and
putting a lid on wisdom?
Many are so forsaken, lost to all possibilities of
ever reaching heaven,
They have lost all hope of ever achieving a
worthwhile goal in life,
Hell will not have mercy on the deceiving, nor
the continuing to deceive.
Discontent will rage through their hearts stifling
all hopes of love.

Many hearts have been broken with all the
disappointments of lost love.
Despair drives them mad, fear blinds them losing
the vision of aspiration,
Losing reason, denying rational thought we close
the gates of wisdom,
Deception holding hands with ignorance march
the whole world to deceive.
However, many are still holding on with every bit
of strength they have for life,
Knowing the future lies with the children
teaching them the way to heaven.

With all out disappointments, folly and
achievements the dream of heaven
Eludes us causing the most grief, it baffles more
than the mystery of love.
Besides hope, there is nothing greater to have, to
possess in this our life.
Hope guides us, love drive us to heaven,
rekindling all our aspirations,
This insight will enlighten us to gain the
understanding to seek wisdom.
When the gates of heaven are opened it will open
the eyes of the deceived.

We must become aware, of all the conflicting
thought passing for wisdom.
Everyone seems to have an opinion of what is
right or wrong about heaven,
This is how we come to all the confusion, and we
all end truly deceived,

Starving for attention, affection, demanding from
others, never giving love.
This is how philosophers and deluded religions
deceive our credulous aspirations.
If it weren't for the confabulators we could be
living a truthful, joyous life.

It's comforting, in spite of all the ambiguity, we
joyously all cling to life,
Equivocation is the devise used by those, as
mirrors to blatantly deceive,
We are not fallen beyond redemption, we must
hold on to our aspirations,
And although the roads are blocked, dark and
dreary, we'll reach our heaven.
We are slowly learning all the intricate and
rewarding ways to give love.
We are awakening to the understanding we
cannot live without wisdom.

Of all gifts wisdom is said the greatest, but who
has tried to live without love,
We will find he has deceived himself and lost the
guidance of all his aspirations,
The secret of life is to live in love discerning, the
wisdom coming from heaven.

THE ABSOLUTE TRUTH

It's not reason that has failed us,
It's us who have failed to reason!
Somehow we have lost track of the God Mind,
Our ship flounders on the reefs of time,
Of deception, deceit, ignorance, greed,
Hatred!

We are so entangled with the vicissitudes of life,
The weeds, we have no time to smell the roses,
To see the brilliance of the sun on the horizon!

We have alternatives and choices to make,
We can continue living in the swamps or,
Live on the Pure Land of the Buddha Mind.
Or fly on Angel's wings to open the gates
Of Heaven, with the God Mind!

THE BUDDHA MIND

The Buddha mind
When it is found,
Has no temporal dimension;
It is longer than long,
Wider than wide,
Higher than high
Yet has no shape or form—
No beginning, no end!

Those who have found it
Can't tell you why—
When!

Many labor all life-long,
Travel far and wide
And find it hard to find
Its trace or its trend.

Some however have found
The Buddha mind
Contemplating a rose,
Kicking a stone,
Meditating a blade of grass.
Whoever you may be,
Wherever you may be going,
You'll know when you've found it,
And mountains won't stand in your way.

You'll walk in silence, but never alone—
Buddha goes, wherever you go.

When we kick a stone,
We should be extra careful,
We may stump a toe,
Be abruptly enlightened!

Buddha is not a careless companion.

Have you seen morning clouds
Reflecting on a mirror lake?
An instant thought you touched the sky.
Have you seen reflected mountains?
Thought they are there to climb.
These are instant reflections of
The Buddha mirror mind!
Because we don't understand this,
We desecrate the mind.
Taking reflected images for reality.

The Buddha mirror mind
Is like a Crystal Lake reflecting
Every passing thought as a cloud,
Through all the fog it sparkles with the sun.
Below it's always liquid crystal clear,
Thoughts on the surface ripples make,
But nothing perturbs the serenity of
The Buddha mirror mind!
It will reflect the sun for all eternity.
Do we dare open the Nirvana gate?
To go, and to be gone beyond
All our thoughts and daily cares.

The light shines everywhere,
To read between the lines,
For those who can, and care!
Free from discriminating thoughts
Consciousness pure, brilliantly clear.
Of all the sacred worlds to build,
All will come from a sacred mind;
The power of Nirvana is within,
All we dare do is touch it!

The Buddha mind encompasses all things,
Yet its not composed of any of them.
The Absolute, the Infinite and the Eternal
Arise from it, yet its beyond all of them.
When the self dissolves, we are one with it.
With equanimity and mindfulness let
The "I" into the emptiness of the void resolve.

Don't raise a thought, an impulse
By intention move, not a grain of sand.
When the self dissolves and the blue
Ethereal clouds; the light will outline
The Divine and the Sacred everywhere!
Live with empathy and compassion,
Neither in aversion nor attachment,
For all the living things in the world.

In the expanse of Nirvana there're mansions
Of heavens where the imagination stills.

THE GOD MIND

The Absolute
The Infinite
The Eternal
Are concepts
Of the Mind.
The beautiful
And
The ugly
Are creations
Of the Mind,
So is
Love and hate
War and peace
Belief and faith
Life and death.
The stars the galaxies
All as they are
From the Mind
Originate.
Nor questions
Or problems
Or solutions
Without
The Mind.
With the Mind
Of God

We can
On Earth
Paradise regain!
When we identify
With the God-mind
Nothing matters as
We are face to face
With immortality!

II

ENLIGHTENMENT

Enlightenment is not that we should achieve
something,
It's that we effortlessly should let go of all
obstructing
The free flow of the light. There is nothing to
attain!
We cannot gain that which from all eternity we
have.
We are but to let it freely flow, as its wills.

The fact is that our spiritual selves are deeper,
Encompassing the entire Universe of existence,
Whereas our physical bodies are finite and
Circumscribed—limited by thought manifest.
Conditioned life is constrained
By the thoughts we think, whereas,
The Absolute is fathomless
Without the constraints of thought.

When the spirit arise to the forefront of
consciousness,
We discern the impermanence of the material.
We see,
The fusion of the Absolute to the concrete.
The concrete spread in space over time
disintegrates,
The Absolute true to its nature, forever continues
Filling the emptiness of the void.

III

THE PERCEPTION OF OUR EXISTENCE

It is said, by many wise men, in Scriptures
written,
Detachment is the way to a Spiritual life.
But we must read, between the lines to find
The way the wise men tell detachment to define.
Meditating on every written line insightfully
given;
Detachment is not only from an ego-self,
With all its wants, desires, possessions craving;

But detachment must also be at a level spiritual,
It's detachment from our self-concept, from that
Which we think we are, to our self-identifying
power—
That sense of self which knows it has no
beginning or end,
Nor shape or form, pigment of skin, gender to
render!
In detachment we don't lose anything but gain

The infinite perspective of our existence!

That entity, which says from all eternity,
My body, my brain, my mind,
Identifies to be that, which it is not,
It defines itself by saying, I am, that I am,
But subsists beyond; it indwells without shape or
form;
An illusory, transient world
But reflects its existence!

It's detachment of our all prevailing
Consciousness self, from the electro-
Magnetic field of energy we assimilate
To make and project our reality.

IV

TO GOD IT WON'T

Would it make a difference if we drank
Sacramental wine from a plastic cup,
Not from a Golden Chalice?
To us it does,
To God it doesn't!

Would it make a difference if we worshipped
God in the open air,
Not from a Luxurious Cathedral?
To us it does,
To God it won't!

Begging The Question

Would it make a difference if we Retreat
At the riverside,
Not at a Ritzy Resort?
To us it does,
To God it won't!

Would it make a difference if the Rosary was said
From memory of the heart,
Not from counting beads?
To us it does,
To God it won't

Would it make a difference if the "Sermon on the
mount"
Was preached at a lakeside,
Not from a mountain peak?
To us it does,
To God it won't!

Would it matter if we openly gather to worship,
Or silently worship in our hearts?
To us it does,
To God it doesn't

Would it matter if the choir singing were
A flock of birds?
To us it does,
To God it won't!

In vain we pilgrimage
The four corners of the earth,
If God we don't
Carry with us!

V

HEAVEN ON EARTH

Fantasizing and ruminating through the corridors
of imagination,
Stumbling on all sorts of surprises, pleasant and
unpleasant,
The mind confabulates seeking closure
rationalizes.

It deeply etches jungle trails of muddy tangled
emotions,
Sensational worlds of conflicting thoughts,
dogmas and weird opinions.
Within these worlds imprisoned, there is no hope
of ever escaping.
Chained remained until we unshackle from the
phantasmagorical fantasies.
Heaven on earth create with the God Mind!

Imagination is the sixth dimension,
In imagination we live most of the time.
Through the power of creative imagination
An imaginary world we've created, and
Our sense of self and the Universe expand.

VI

THE INFINITE PRESENCE

When God infuses my being with His Presence,
The brilliance of the sun dims by His Light.
I must avoid every miniscule impulse of thought
Which hinders His Love, burning in my heart!
The instance I raise a thought to say I am,
The I separate from
The great beyond!

I need not think of the path the saints have trod;
Neither philosophy nor science outshines His
Light,
Nor all the prayers and rosaries forever said—the
fringe
Of a shadow can't wedge His love from my
heart!

Nor, can my finite intellect comprehend His.
But, we need not the intellect if we have His
Love!
Love is the most potent power we humans have;
The intellect makes us bright, love Godlike!

God's Consciousness manifests everywhere,
It's us, who have lost awareness of It.
To regain His Consciousness clear the mind of
debris;
If we clear our hearts of ignorance, greed and
hatred,
It will glow with His Infinite Presence!

The forever Knowing, Omniscient Mind of God
Without shape or form knows

What the finitude of the human mind only
surmises!
We may Psychologize, Theologize, Hypostatize,
But, only with the God Mind
Can we detach from our finite self,
To Know more, Love more, Be more!

The apprehension and discovery of Quantum
Physics,
As the underling force manifesting the Universe,
Is man's supreme discovery, but only when,
Our consciousness makes a quantum leap
To the Consciousness of God, we observe
The world,
Retransformed!

What privilege it is to be, co-creators of our
Universe!
And Heaven is the most awe-inspiring
architecture
Of the human mind;
A greater marvel outshining the physical
mansions
Of earth we've created!

The "God Concept" is the most sublime,
By virtue evolved from the human mind.
The "Big Bang Theory" is just what
It is, a cosmic puff of passing wind;
It nowhere begins, in a "black hole" ends!

The Mystic Embodiment Of Love

The moment of revelation
Is the moment I opened my eyes and—before me
you stood!
Ere, my life meant nothing but sorrow. O, joyous
Anticipation!
Without a glance I know your fragrance,
For never have I inhaled a rose as fragrant, or
seen beauty rare, as the
Night unexpected by my bed you stopped and
whispered,
Breathing persuasively in my ear: I am the
dream you dream about!

I'll return and recur, again and again occur, until
love you've gained.

You declared!
I am the reason for your existence
And my existence is the reason you exist:
The deifying dialectic theorem of my existence,
Dogma beyond dogmas, the sacred beyond
adulation!

Was this for real? Was I dreaming, scarcely
believing,
I ask: Who are you to wrench my heart with
agony so great,

A love beyond sublime, impossible to define?
Asking nothing in return, but give what I will.

Friends or enemies whoever can tell: says, to
peruse you is mad,
For you are not right, imprisoning my soul.
They say you'll make demands no human can,
endure!
To hear your songs I must rise early in the
morning,
Must seclude myself in silence to hear your
whispering
Love in my ears, and the beat of your heart in
mine.
Must shun all engaging in ethereal connubial
love. Worldly pleasures deny
To enjoy your euphoric warmth, your refulgent
light—effulgent beyond
The mighty sun.

And you are here again, to torment—love
torments!
Your absence is excruciating torture intense.
You are the dilemma of my life!
Overtures to my intellect overwhelms, my
emotional soul submissive,
My beliefs do injustice to my reason! You're
Love persistent!
I know you are of a dimension I can't grasp—
head dumbfounded, derisive,
Heart dense weakly aspiring. Finitely suffocating,
in your absence I can't Exist!

The stars reflecting in your eyes confuse the beat
of my heart,
Confounding my senses, I hear your smile and
see the songs
You speak. You are the fruit in the orchard
forbidden to eat!
The Gardenia in the garden—enticed to touch,
As the stars and the moon has always been.
The mystic Embodiment of Love!
Beauty, and good of all angels ever from heaven
to come,
Those who come are but your shadow, sent.

Hard as I try to forget, hence that night, I sense
your presence standing there,
An invisible radiance nudging, following
everywhere!
Your absence makes me mad, your presence
always glad,

Your negation despair!

So enamored I am, life matters not!
But what must I, a mortal do,
Die to embrace you?

Must your embrace be the cause of my death?
But to love should not be to die—It's ignorance
and pride that kills,
And arrogance will bury its dead!

O, spontaneous mystical experience! Divine
Mystery unexplained!

Your whispered love in my ear, endures,
Allays my sorrow, my fear of death.

My heart expectant craves your love in excess,
Your every touch hungers my soul, ever more,
Lights a resplendent fire burning, aglow.

O! Devine Presence transmuting,
Base metal to gold—the commonplace turns
altars to adore!
Will Thou my mind enlighten as Thou my soul
possess?
I, who cannot myself define, can I be defined in
You?
The fires in my heart lit, burns bright—
sometimes dismayingly, ever so low,
Intuitive faith
forevermore!

Enlightenment is the awareness of a
Transcendent conscious awareness
That pervades and motivates all things.
An awareness beyond absolute existence,
Beyond infinite space and eternal time;
Attunement with the crystal clear mind. Beyond
Our thoughts; the glitter of the world.

THANKFUL FOR THE GIFT

Humility puts us in a frame of mind,
To serve everyone. Contentment,
Makes a treasure a crumb of bread.
Reverence makes us kneel to adore
The stars, for their everlasting presence.
Gratitude makes us thankful for the gift
Of life given, unconditionally to share!

Let not arrogance mar this grandness,
As we voyage through the avenues of life. And
But in solemn prayer repeat these treasures
For the whole world to hear:
Humility!
Contentment!
Reverence!
Gratitude!

WHO TAUGHT THE BIRDS TO FLY

Across the oceans birds fly to nest
In exotic and foreign lands. Why!
Who taught them to fly, caring for
Their young? It's not the merchantmen
Who rode the seas. They didn't come
To nest. They came to rip the chest
Of all the maidens they can see. Against
Their will, they tear, slash and slit
The throats of all the men they encounter.
Armored with shields of mal-intention,
They converge with hostile disagreement,
Stealing all the treasure of the land.
The birds only leave an empty nest;
When they return their offspring fly
Back with them. The merchantmen
Leave sperms crawling in abandonment,
And all the minds and virgins raped!
Their wake as a tidal wave perish
The land to desolate barren desert.
They show no sorrow, hold no vigil,
Over the corpse they leave to inter.
Who taught the birds to fly, to cross
The oceans? To build a nest again?
Who taught the invaders, crusaders,
Of foreign countries to leave a legacy
Of destruction—the birds do fly!

Begging The Question

Who taught the birds to fly
Leaving no destruction?

WHY THE BIRDS FLY

When the birds fly,
They don't fly in an empty sky.
When the fish swim,
They don't swim in an empty ocean.
They are just like you and me,

We fly the skies, swim the oceans
Filled with a radiant presence from
The mystical grandeur of the cosmos,
The omnipresent mystery of God—
The magnificence of our humanity!

We are witnessing participators
 Of splendors, we know not from
Whence their sublimity originate.
We walk the earth, look at the sky
Vaguely, ignorant of what we are.

To feel the Divinity of God,
We must see the sacredness of things
Merging the mystical to the mundane.
Take not God as a whim, a passing cloud,
Nor our lives, live, as a puff of wind.

To remember to remember ourselves
Through the power of mindfulness,

Is to forever be in God's presence;
How can we be wrong, or do wrong!

A Narrative Exposition Of
THE ABSOLUTE TRUTH

Let's see if we can also restate some of these truths from a psychological perspective, using the language of science. All our hatred, anger, frustration, jealousy, depression and destructive behavior come from a judgmental call, which we express to ourselves in a simple statement: That persons, things, circumstances and events are, or are not, the way we think they should be. Our expectation of what or how we think they should be, and not accepting them for what they are in themselves, unconditionally, is the cause of all our confusion, misery and pain.

The laws of physics are inviolable and are always seeking balance and equilibrium. Everything that can happen does, and only can happen within the constraints of the laws of physics; nothing happens outside of the Universe. If it happens, it's because it can happen the way it happens, not the way we think it should.

The converse is true, if things happen, and we think that's the way it should happen, we are joyful, happy and contented. We do have the power to change things, by the way, we think of them. We are not affected by things, but by our reaction to them. In any instance of time, in the past, the present or the future, as the world is viewed so it is. We make our reality by our thoughts, outside of thought there is only a potentiality, ready to be molded into our world by the power of our thoughts. As the waves of the electromagnet field impinge upon our sense organs, the brain interprets them as our world, and projects them. The universe as we know it is from a human perspective, and is limited by the limits of our senses, sight, hearing, touch, smell, taste, feelings and understanding. Therefore, each conscious being lives in his Universe.

Nevertheless, in the Universe in itself, there are no intrinsic or extrinsic values, except what we impute and attribute to things, because they are conducive to our sense-of-well-being and to our survival. To live an ethical and moral life is just as necessary for our survival, as it is to inhale clean air and drink uncontaminated   water.
Whether we are conscious of it or not, the human organism is always seeking homeostasis. To achieve this it is necessary to live an honest, balanced life as an enlightened, Genuine Human Being.

Our sense-of-self which we acquire as we become self-conscious, never changes, and remains with us from birth to death. And perhaps even beyond death, but we have no way of proving this. What we do know is that every element, every energy unit as molecules and atoms of our being returns to the universal field. Our sense-of-self is our self-identifying-power which, becomes submerged by a maze of thoughts, beliefs and opinions, but nevertheless, in it, remains untainted, pure, and brilliantly transparent. This self-identifying principle, the knowing principle and the life principle are one and the same. We cannot have one without the other, and when they move out of themselves, upon themselves an existence arises.

Freud calls this self-identifying power the Id, except that for him; it is unconscious, and this hodgepodge of thoughts, feelings and beliefs we hold, the Ego. In reality, there is no Id, or ego as an entity, anywhere to be found. The Ego has become the scapegoat for all our irresponsible behavior; we even have developed whole systems of thought about this idea, as egotistic, egoism, egocentrism. This is another example, of how we develop systems of thought around our misperceptions and mistaken beliefs. The truth of the matter is, that by the time we reach the age of six our character is formed; we have acquired a core of conditioned responses, mental, emotional and physical to cope with the world. However, that doesn't mean it cannot be changed; furthermore, as we grow, and mature, we acquire new skill and knowledge. And by early adulthood, our frontal cortex has developed to give to give us our cognitive faculties and sense of discretion and responsibility.

In conclusion, it is true that traces of our brutish Neanderthal ancestry still linger with us, but man is more so a spiritual being, then a physical being. For as we regress from the molecular elements of our being to the atom, we find that the atom breaks further down to units of energy scientists call Quanta, which we cannot define as waves or particles, and have no beginning or end. This is what we are, from a psychological and scientific point of view—any question?

Let's see if we can make the connection between the scientific and the theological. In the poem, THE GOD MIND, you'll find these lines: "When we identify with the God-mind, nothing matters as, we are in person with immortality." This metaphor translates to, when we regress to the organ systems, which constitutes the human organism, to the tissues, cells, molecules, atoms, and to the quanta of energy, we find this energy is infinite and eternal—we can also say immortal. And we really don't find an individual "Self". That which we term, the "soul" is a quantum of energy, which to date, we have no scientific proof how it manifests; and it's a theological assumption; not a scientific fact.

Let's take another line from the poem, THE INFINITE PRESENCE: "The instant I raise a thought to say I am, the I separate from, the great beyond." This is a metaphor for, every time we raise a thought to think about us, things or the Universe in general; we must use an image, imagination, a sound or vocalization to symbolically represent what we are thinking about—this creates a dichotomy. Think about this, what is out there, are clusters of energy we term Electromagnetism, Gravity, Weak and Strong forces, but even these, are concepts of the mind? Therefore, what we think we see and know are an interpretation and projection by the Human brain. Without a self-conscious brain, the universe as we know it does not exist. The brain is a dynamo transformer of energy; it inputs and output's energy, transforming it to a world we desire and visualize. And each of us lives, and can only live at the level of our understanding; and our perspective of the world, is limited by that understanding.

Mind is energy use it creatively; thought is mental power in action, but it can be constructive or destructive. It has created highways and tunnels through mountains, dammed mighty rivers, flight in the air and instant communication across the globe, but it has also created wars and atom bombs.

We are all connected through a conscious life principle. Therefore, we can say, we are all interconnected by a universal energy source. Mindfulness is a conscious-awareness state whereby we can see and feel this connection. This is the process by or through which energy becomes conscious of itself—it becomes conscious energy. This is a simplification of how energy becomes not only conscious energy, but also conscious of itself.

And the big question is: How does this vast, endless field of energy begin? That's where the limits of our understanding find closure in the God concept; and the "Big-Bang Theory" which is just another dead end. The Human Intellect seems not capable of knowing the beginning, nor the end, or of knowing its limits. That's why "Faith" is such a huge sell. There are so many frontiers to cross. However, all we know as of now is speculation, assumption regressing upon another assumption. Even all the marvels we have accomplished, by harnessing the laws of nature, they are all within the constraint of the human intellect. An aside, (don't get me wrong, I am not knocking Faith down; for faith is a strong motivational force, humans have. Faith and hope fits like a glove to a hand. It is Hope which provides the drive to survive, but it is faith, which provides the spiritual fortitude to overcome the obstacles we encounter in life. Faith does not necessarily have to be of a religious belief, but a belief in us, and the potentially of our humanity.)

Consider the following statements from science: It is said, everything in the Universe is in constant movement. However, movement, to be detected as movement must move against something static, which is not moving. Therefore, there must be an unmoving knowing principle in the Universe. This was postulated by Thomas

Aquinas, Italian Theologian, 1225-1274. Physicists call it the Higgs field, interpreted by some as a mind-field. Theologians, reverently call it God!

It is said that things cannot move greater than the speed of light, which is approximately 186,282 miles per second. However, that which can conceptualize light traveling at this speed, must be greater than light. Who or what is the perceiver—the static observer of light traveling through the air? It is said that the Universe is expanding, where is it expanding to, is it space, where does this space come from? If there is infinite space, that from which it originates and knows it, must be greater than infinite space? But, what can we postulate greater than infinite space? I think, it can be said. Everything in the Universe has a cognitive component, and otherwise, it does not exist.

Scientists tell us there are more dimensions, besides our three dimensional physical world of length, breadth and depth. They also tell us about parallel Universes, which are reflections, or duplications of our Universe, even duplications of individual humans with all their idiosyncratic traits. These are, at best, mathematical models, which are difficult for untrained, everyday, minds to understand. Physics also consider 'Time" the fourth dimension, saying that everything occurring must do so through a span of time. However, I would say we must have space, before we have time, for space is the medium through which time travels. Time, is the duration it takes an object, without taking velocity into account, to move from one point in space to another. The concepts of length, breadth, depth, space and time are limitless. I would rather think that space is the fourth dimension and time the fifth. I would also like to postulate that the sixth dimension is imagination, which is also limitless. Come to think of it, it is through imagination; we conceptualize all the other dimensions, our Universe with its galaxies, and the entire parallel Universe with their galaxies.

Let's talk some more about imagination being an important dimension of our existence, and see why. About ninety-nine percent of our world is imaginary; the other one percent is lived in an area of space enclosed by three-dimensional objects. However, even these are limited by our sensory system. We can only see a limited range of light, hear a limited range of sound, the same it is with touch. We can only live within a certain range of atmospheric pressure and temperature. This is where imagination fills in. Therefore, we live in a fully rounded world, everything we know, or we think about our world, us and the Universe, and the parallel universe is the work of imagination.

We also cover the world with an emotional blanket, and numerous disciplines of thought. Some are in accord and reflect reality. Some don't. Not all our belief systems are valid, for many of them are based on myth and superstition, if we come to think about it, superstition is deeply woven in the fabric of our societies and culture. Many outmoded beliefs and cultures are still lingering on, in spite of developments in modern culture, and intellectual advancements. However, in the development of our cultures, moral relativism must not be allowed to take the place of conscience, and as mentioned before morality and ethical conduct are innate dispositions necessary for our survival.

It's said that what the mind of man can conceive, the mind of man can achieve. However, it also must be said that all we have achieved, all the arts, and sciences, philosophies and beliefs are the product of imagination. It's through the power of imagination; we have transformed the world. Evolution is not only a physical process, because it has also evolved the mind, and the mind has helped transform the world to our liking. Even so, of all the wonderful things we've created with imagination, we've also created beautiful fairytales of make-belief; we clothe these with unshakable belief, and parade them with unfathomable faith. Here is something else to think about: What we want is what we get, because only what we visualize for ourselves, we deserve, nothing more nothing less.

I think it would be appropriate if we talk about detachments here, in the poem THE

PERCEPTION OF OUR EXISTENCE, I said, "But detachment must also be at a level spiritual....It's detachment of our prevailing consciousness self; from the electromagnetic field, we assimilate, to make and project our reality." I want you to take note that we are not talking about resignation, which is negative, whereas detachment is positive. The word spiritual is also an abstract concept, an intuitive notion we have about ourselves being something more than our physical bodies. When we refer to ourselves as spiritual, we usually have the feeling that our spiritual self is an ethereal body, which is more, and detached, but in and out of our physical bodies—also, that our physical body is a poor manifestation of it. If we equate spiritual to energy, this makes sense.

Above, I have also said that imagination fills out our sense of self, and our sense of the Universe, where our senses fall short. Somewhere else, I have furthermore said that our everyday accepted perception is that there is a Universe, and consciousness arises out of it; however, that the contrary is true, there is consciousness and our perception of the Universe arise out of it. There is a collective all pervading consciousness and what we know of ourselves, and the Universe arises from it. A Universe without consciousness-awareness does not make sense.

Maybe an example would help us to understand detachment, when we go to see a movie in a theater; we are sitting in anticipation for the movie to begin, within a few moments after the movie starts, we become completely detached from ourselves, and identified with the characters, the setting and storyline of the movie, oblivious of our surrounding. When the movie ends, we return to our reality, from the artificial reality we became merged to. Later if we want, through the power of memory, we can recall scenes from the movie and project those on our consciousness screen. If we grasp this, we'll see that our existence is just a movie we have projected out of our brain, and we are so identified with it, we don't know, we can detach from it—all it takes is a paradigm shift, a Gestalt flip. The problem is our movie doesn't end. We have to detach from it, and see it for what it is, and then we can have control over it. If the drama of our life is not filled with laughter and joy, why not rewrite the script?

In the poem, "WHY THE BIRDS FLY" there is a line, "We are witnessing participators of splendors; we know not from, whence their sublimity originates." Through the power of memory, we are in constant identification with our movie. The object of detachment would be to become witnessing participators, by standing aside, as it were, and enjoy ourselves, watching the movie. Life is indeed a movie in constant movement, flashing nanosecond by nanosecond across the screen of consciousness; it can also be said, life is a poem; we live by metaphor.

Nevertheless, I would like to leave you with some more conundrums, or enigmas. I call them brain-teasers: When we talk about the Ultimate Reality, we say, it must be Absolute, Infinite and Eternal. However, the Absolute must know itself absolutely, otherwise it's not absolute. The Infinite must know itself infinitely, otherwise it's not infinite. The Eternal must know itself eternally, otherwise it's not eternal. However, we must not lose track of the Perceiver. Who or what perceives all this "knowing." May it not just be energy becoming conscious of it? The perceiver is "that" within us, which perceives; it has no shape or form, nor beginning or end—it comes into existence in the act of pure perceiving— that's when we may catch glimps of it. It's that power which impulses us to move and act intentionally on the Universe.

A concept arises from the Human mind and if the mind can grasp and comprehend it, then the mind is beyond its concepts. Likewise, Existence to exist, must know it exists; something must know it exists, otherwise it does not exist. I'll repeat, a universe without conscious-awareness does not make sense. Therefore, the supreme principle in the Universe is conscious-awareness, from which intelligence and reasoning arise.

Any other beings throughout the Universes must have these attributes, or greater, perhaps even some, we cannot be beginning to relate to. If we meditate on these, it will expand our comprehension beyond the restraints of logic. Understanding is our capacity for rational thought, and takes place against a backdrop of perpetual knowing, which is beyond our understanding. Comprehension is an intuitive grasp of knowledge without the prop of the senses. It's to see a deeper meaning and relationship between the things we apprehend.

I would like to leave you with that inner calm assurance that the Universe is of you, as much as you are of the Universe. Moreover, that the mind is greater than its concepts because they arise out of it. Therefore, all we know of ourselves, the Universe and our place in it are only concepts of the mind. "All that we are, is the result of what we have thought," and if we want to change ourselves and the world all we have to do is change our thoughts. It is proven in psychology, and in physics that our thoughts affect the structure of the brain, and the structure of the brain affects our thoughts. Furthermore, that the brain has a certain plasticity, which means that the brain can regenerate itself and learn new things, no matter how old we are.

Implicit in the concept of evolution is the notion it has no end. It does not have an end, nor can we stop it. We can help it along, perhaps sidetrack it, but only as far as it would let us. It was also necessary to its process to develop self-conscious life that can reflect upon itself and reproduce itself. And above all, the miracles of the human brain organ which can introspect, know, counsel and repair it. And, even destroy it.

That the mind is greater than its thoughts can be grasped if we introspect on these statements: There is a thought transcending awareness that permeates and motivates thought; there is a feeling transcending awareness that permeates and motivates feelings; there is a behavior transcending awareness that permeates and motivates behavior. The mind can know itself without its thoughts, but the moment; we raise a thought about it; it submerges and identifies with the thought. Therefore, the only way the mind knows itself, is through its self-identifying power, stripped from all impulses of thought. The mind does exist without its thoughts, but thoughts cannot exist without the mind. There is a pure consciousness field from which all things originate, yet it is not composed of them; it is transparent, brilliantly bright when freed from discriminating thought. The same it is with God. We cannot know God per se, but by his works, and if we interiorize Him, and let His Being permeate our being by identifying with the God-mind.

Am I writing Eulogies to the wind? It is hard to say, but most of us will not take the time to understand these concepts. Humans in general, do not like to think outside of their comfort zone. We share a strong tendency to lean on an authority figure, real or imaginary, which then control our lives with, or without our consent. Furthermore, each of us lives, and can only live, at the level of our understanding; however, understanding is developmental. All we have to do is open our minds and let information in, in order to be assimilated. Every insight we get expands our horizon, giving us a different perspective. This essay is intended to do just that—open your mind. It can be read at different levels.

GRASPING FOR REALITY

Reality seems to take on many facets
Like rainbows many colors in the air.
Sometimes black as carbon night, or
Bright as sparkling diamond light.

They seem to come and go nowhere.
The illusion mesmerizing our senses,
Delusional with phantoms ghosts
Of another world as with our soul.

In reality we cannot discern the reality
Behind the reality, if it's all a dream!
All our objective views are subjective,

Grasping air, when we grasp to hold!
Yet we dream, dreams no one dares,
Hoping they'll come true, every year!

An open mind fertilizes itself,

With the soil of magnificent thoughts,
Beholding the most beautiful gardens
Of our imagination wrought!

I always write against religious fanaticism, but I must confess I am a fanatic, when it comes to eradicating Ignorance, Greed and Hatred, and replacing them with Wisdom, Benevolence and Compassion—all divine attributes.

NB

Please, don't take this lightly, the reason history repeats itself, is that humans don't learn from history. The major cause of the downfall of all the civilizations, and mighty nations of the world, has been indolence, indulgence, greed, hatred, and ignorance—including, but not limited to, Babylonia, Egypt, Greece, Rome, Great Briton, Germany, and Russia. And if we can read the hand writing on the wall as it is being written, so it will come to be for The United States Of America, if we don't change. Everything said applies to America today. It doesn't take much insight to see there is an undercurrent of corruption and twisted values at all levels of the federal and state governments, the professions, and the professional and legal associations, corporations and service organizations, which will be difficult to reverse. What do you think caused the Enron's, the housing bobble, and the economic collapse? Greed, we must remember is not only for material possessions, but also for the aggrandizement of that illusory entity we call the ego.

Furthermore, deception is so ingrained in our psyche; we don't seem to know right from wrong anymore. It is a contagious disease, which is growing to an epidemic in our societies. People are in the habit of lying, even if telling the truth would be more elegant. And it seems they have fallen into a trap that it's honorable to lie, if telling the truth would expose their inadequacies and deficiencies. Deception is rampant in all walks of life, even among those in authority positions, heads of state, Presidents, CEO's of Corporations, and religious institutions, no matter what denomination they claim to be.

There is no doubt, there is a gap in our psyche, some call it a drive, perhaps it's an emptiness, which needs to know the how and the why of our existence, and that of the Universe. Fortunately, for us, this drive has let us to the discovery of the methodologies of science, and we are coming to an empirical more realistic view of our existence. Before that, it was anyone's game, and as we look back on our history, we find a hodgepodge of contradicting philosophies and religious beliefs; unfortunately, we still find strong elements of these in our societies today, and they influence how we live, how we worship and govern ourselves. However, a good many of us are seeing through the myth and superstition and are guiding our lives accordingly. Nevertheless, these traditions and way of thinking are so woven into our societies it will take another thousand year or more for them to be completely eradicated What do you think would happen if we all start telling the truth? The world would settle into its own reality.

Why is it taking so long for us to come to the full realization that we create ourselves and our world by our thoughts? By our self-concept, we determine who we are; and also, our world and the Universe is only what we think it is. So, since most, everything we've created is flawed, when are we going to change our thoughts and create a more congenial world to live in?

Let us not destroy the Earth, but replenish it; and also in awe wonder at the marvel of the Human Brain. Stand and behold the beauty of where the waters separate from the earth. Walk the beaches with sands between the toes, our gaze outlining the horizon, and our consciousness, "Filled with the radiant presence from, the mystical grandeur of the cosmos, the omnipresent mystery of God, the magnificence of our Humanity"—fly with the birds in Humility! Contentment! Reverence! Gratitude!

I have asked you to "Please, don't take it lightly"; and I have said, "It could prove to be therapeutic for humanity." Reading thus far, I hope you have gained the insights I was pointing out. Now, I am humbly asking you to pay attention. Why attention? Because, "Attention" and "Intention" are two powers, humans have, which separates us from all the other species on the planet, and perhaps in the Universe. Without the power of intention and attention, we cannot even move a little finger. We may intend to do something, but it never gets done, without the intentional impulse to get it done. We cannot move or do anything without attention and intentionally applying the power of intention to move it or get it done. Without attention, we are zombies living in limbo. When we are paying attention to something, it integrates with us; holding it in conscious/awareness, all our senses act and interact with it; it becomes our reality. And if we don't intentionally keep our attention on it, holding it in awareness, it does not exist for us. We are only what we are holding in attention; we are the thoughts, the feeling, the sensations, the beliefs we allow to flash across the screen of conscious/awareness. We are what we are experiencing. Our minds and bodies are pure, clean energy, they become contaminated by ego formation and our self-concept. These with attention and intention we can change.

WHAT A WONDERFUL MACHINE

What a wonderful machine
The Universe is!
It precisely the condition sustains
Necessary for life to spring,
From spring to spring.

What a wonderful machine
A Human Being is!
It's made of atom strings
Without identity,
But finds its own.

What a wonderful machine
The human brain is!
Without ever been told how,
It considers far more
Than it weighs.

What a wonderful machine
The human eye is!
It distinguishes dark from light
It matters not how fast
The speed of light is.

What a wonderful machine
The human heart is!

It circulated to sustain life,
Finding love where there is none,
To forever love.

What wondrous mystery
The Universe is!
It contains dimensions
We are yet to know,
And many we'll never know.

What a wonderful machine
The Universe is!
And all that wherefrom springs.

SAID THE BUTTERFLY

What have I made of my life?
Said the Butterfly,
Flying through the air.

Found a destination,
Having an affaire with the atoms,
Hitchhiking through the air.

What I've done said the Butterfly,
Flying through the air,
Merged beauty with the reflected sun.

What I've done said the Butterfly,
Appreciate every breath of air.
That's why 'am significant!

It's what I did with life
Important, not just to fly,
Said the Butterfly!

FINALE

NOTHING BUT THE TRUTH

When I express my thoughts in poetic lines,
Scientists say their hypothetical expositions are
truer than mine.
And I also wonder why? Yonder,

Theologians standing against an impenetrable
wall,
Proclaim their dogmas are truer than what I've
rhymed?
To be guilty of perjury would be futile and
pathetic, but they do it!

Truth cannot be truer than it is, neither exposed
by Degrees,
Nor by favored scribes, transcribed for generation
to come.
None is privileged to know more, than we all can
ever know.

Perhaps, there is no truth at all, it depends on our
perspective!
Beauty is only as beauty is perceived—so it could
be,
For all promulgated dogmatic opinions and
scribbling!

PATRIARCH OF LOTUS-EATERS

I question not why I am!
Nor why I am not,
given the talents of the wise maidens.

What I bitterly rally the gods about,
why I am left out the gates of heaven?
Given no alternative but:
Forfeiture of will for obedience.

What determinism is left me,
in a field of submissive celestial orbs?
Would chaos be more becoming, than the fires of
hell?

Wines of musky taste in ancient goblets served,
gold has not been found, they were made of lead,
garlands of platitudes adorns my head.
What other wisdom-hidden parables should be
said?
Holy threats to my mind, faints my hearts'
concern.

I am not the Prodigal Son. My brother is,
he squandered the fortunes of the Kingdom,
returning to the Father empty headed, mockingly
repentant,

Shielded by the meshes of the confessional.
Prophesying from visitations of his mind
frustrating, annoying catastrophic happening.

If we didn't bring offerings to replenish the
Kingdom,
he said I prophecy: Tribulations on top of
tribulations
for generations to come. These are well written,
and as written shall be done:

There will be wars into the far distance of time,
ultramodern in design without cause or end.
They shall rage beyond the valleys to the shrines,

For the wrath of the gods furies hearts of men.
In the name of the Father and a place in Heaven,
brother shall slay brother, as did Cain to Abel.

They shall peruse the scriptures from cover to
cover
until the pages are shred, and in ignorance
remain.
They shall walk in the absence of wisdom
until the Arctic ice melts, and the lands are
submerged,
Until the waters of Niagara cease their eternal
fall,
and the boundaries of reason turn pillars of salt!

And the Father forgave him for saying these
things,

saying: Well said my son, and each species shall
live
 in their realm and multiply.

Only man transgresses violating all.
I will give you for the omniscience displayed,
the keys of the castle on yonder hill.

And it's decreed the slaves remain as slaves
to serve you, for it would embolden them
to know that but for thought they would own
the kingdom and the land around them.

It's also decreed all the maidens of the land,
not only the foolish ones,
prostrating themselves prostitute before you.

For it is not good for a man to light a fire alone,
a seed cast on barren land bears no fruit.
But it is good for a man that he should lay
many times as he can to fertilize the land.

Bring forth children as many as swarms
of locust to ravish the land. No destiny foretold.
Let the grasshoppers munch down the trees,
pollute the skies raving mad.

Am I the Patriarch of all those lotus-eaters,
drug peddlers, and criminals?

MAXIMS ARE DOGMAS

An ephemeral description
Makes not for consolation
When the figure of speech
Is from mouths of the dumb.

Aphoristic expressions may
Contain truism if they are
Rightly understood, but
Will never die if repeatedly
Proclaimed to be wisdom.

So conjecture can be more
Than an assumption, it can
Be an occasion for humor.

But, maxims can be dogmas
Disguise proclaiming souls
Of the living, and or dead.

Lauding words glorifying,
Extolling, exalting divinities:
Sculptured from thin air!

Saints by dozens canonized,
Faux statues witness to faith,
In assumed delusive heavens.

Best place to rest—headstones,
An epigraph on a tombstone
Well written—is the best advice.

PROPHESY ACCURATELY

Of all the destinies man self-predict:
Said by the prophets of antiquity
In tones of certainty resounding thru time,
Eloquently said in flowing words,
Alleged to be from high authority.
Unfortunately lacking accuracy,
Never a line of which, a word comes true.

Anticipated many centuries ago,
Waited in times gone by, and times to come
For that promised land of bees and honey.
We got a crucified messiah
Whose death promises an eternal heaven?
Will this prophet's promise come to pass?
To redeem this death? Our crucifying him!

Why can't we prophesy accurately!

FIGHTING STARS TO NO END

I am what I am and should be
Don't tell me what I should be,
For then both you and I will break bones,
Opening chest of scars that don't mend,
Fighting stars to no end.

So the swirls of desert dust
Mistaken for swarms of birds.
And reptile's fusil tongues streaking
Mistaken for falling meteorites,
Fighting stars to no end.

Don't tell me what I should be,
For I am what I am to no end.
Wearing scars that don't mend!
Strokes of lightening in inky heads.
Excursions of arching dendrites

When the final leap is made
Across cracks of sun baked land,
Reptile's recoil to whatever shade they find,
The stars must be forgiven for
Failing to fill our empty heads.

LEAP OF FAITH

This is my Universe, which from folds in my
cranium unfurls,
It's mine and mine alone. The spinning galaxies
from my mind,
Made from particles eons floating through space
and time.

This is my Universe, which with a blink appears
or disappears,
As ingrained impressions from my point of
observation. But
We beg the question: Is it a leap of faith, or a
quantum stare?

Gaping and gazing, as far as eyes can go,
returning from nowhere
Empty as the void can be. All monuments from
stones are made,
Heads filled with spinning galaxies, leaps of
faith, nothing more!

This is my soul, never from molecule strands
compounded,
It's not mine nor mine alone, made from thoughts
eons floating

Through space and time, myths spanned from
ancestral minds.

Universes from chaos we spin, imputing them
law and order,
Projecting stars, classifying them against an
empty infinite sky,
Wondering how, why, we touch them only with a
quantum sigh?

AD INFINITUM

When I question myself ad infinitum,
I find myself expanding, with an expanding
Universe,
I find myself riding, revolving clouds of
dilemmas.
Really never ever having found my identity,
I really don't know who I am!

I really never knew who, or where I came from,
Or where I am suppose to go; and the places I am
Told to, are neither here, nor in the Universe—Ad
Infinitum!
And all the other grand ideas I ever had,
Are as illusive, as the ever changing clouds

Riding clouds of dilemmas, we'll never know
why—
Ad Infinitum!

THOUGHTS HAVE SHAPED THE WORLD

Ideas have created great inventions,
Thoughts have shaped and changed the world.
We should have been more careful,
What and how we were thinking?

We are chained, with chains of moral slavery,
Starved by the winds of economic whims,
Led by the nose with rings of herd mentality.
Identity lost, in hero-worshipping, confusing
tongues.

Shouldn't we be heeding to change all the things
that's not working?
Or, all the things went wrong,
Shouldn't we be using the exact ideas? And,
The proper ways of critical thinking?

BY REGRESSION EXPLAINED

Power and magic are the tools we use
To school the young, control the very old
At the start, the middle, the very end.
When they claim we must hear a sermon said.
We imprison all their hopes and their dreams,
In the longest fairytale ever told:

How a magic spell was caste creating
In an instant smaller than nano time
All the galaxies, planets and the stars,
Of how we began from nothing or space
And have a loud explosion-taking place,
In the garden beyond Genesis gate.
Visitations of Angels making hellos
of the stormy, radiating clouds,
predicting inconceivable births
and the rising of the dead.
No one knows the beginning or the end,
of how the smallest grain of sand
is necessary to the expanding Universe.
Or the single life cell can multiply
to the complex human organism.
Only by regression explained!

SAVING THE ART I'VE DONE

With brilliant colors nature paints
Magnificent landscapes for the eyes to see,
With harmonious sounds symphonies of music
For the ears to hear, and the soul's delight.

From the elements of the void she builds
Magnificent galaxies for us to behold
In the dimensions of space she placed
Suns for the planets round to revolve.

With spans of time slowly passing
She stopped volcanoes from erupting,
Separated cooling waters from the land,
Her masterpiece evolved, the infant soul!

Now she rests pensively wondering:
What else dare I do with the void? —
I've make Universes, galaxies and stars,
And Humans who don't care—?

But I am not disappointed in what I've done.
Within the soul I've planted a redemptive
Spark to spread around the world, hourly
Lighting hearts saving the art I've done.

ALL WE HAVE THOUGHT

(In the beginning was the Word
And the Word was with God.)

Consciousness creates reality,
Perception gives it form,
Awareness discriminates between them.
Conscious/awareness is the highest
Attributes of man.
With these he breeds
Volumes of poetry,
Universes galaxies filled
As beautiful as the roses
In gardens nestled by the wind.
They breathe the breath of life
Upon another
Refreshed every spring.

Let's sweep away pretention,
Make a clean, fresh start by
Accepting us unconditionally.

Thank the Heavens for the power
Of thought, the power to think.
To know all we have been,
Will ever be, is what we think.
From moment to moment we are
The sum total of what we have

Allowed ourselves to think.

It's by the power of thought
We'll overcome ignorance,
Greed, hatred and deception,
To make our life on earth a
Happy, contented, joyous one.
Its pretention leads to deception,
We are not really affected by
Things, it's the views of them.

II

The enlightened man is always
in a state of full mindfulness,
Eternally remembering
Himself and all created things
In the forever present now.
At the right hand of the Father
He sits as the Co-creator
Of the Universe and the world.
With peace he watches the birds fly,
The beauty of the clouds unfurl,
Calm the fury of the passions
By the wave of his steady hands.
He sees the transitoriness
Of he idols we adore.
His heart blossoms in compassion
For every grain of sand stepped on.
His desire to free the minds,
Forevermore, of everyone!

THE SPIRIT UNITES

There is a song which says:
"What the world needs now is
Love, sweet love."

I totally agree, and must add
That besides unconditional love,
What the world needs now is
A balanced mind and an open heart.

It's the mind that sees the road,
But it's the heart that guides us,
It's the soul that bears us,
But it's the spirit that unites us!

Its true God gives us free will
And alternatives in life,
But there is one choice He gives,
Which no other alternative has,
To know and believe in Him!

To know Him is to know Him
With our whole mind, without reserve.
To believe in Him is to believe in Him
With our whole heart, without doubt.
We have no other viable choice!

ABOUT THE AUTHOR

Thomas P. Lind is retired; he was Director of Dietary
Services at The New York United Hospital Medical Center
of Port Chester, N. Y., where he also taught classes in
Biofeedback theory and practice at the school of
Encephalography. He has degrees in Psychology. He was
a member of the International College of Applied Nutrition
and of the American Hospital Association, and an
associate member of the Academy of Orthomolecular
Psychiatry. He was a member of the American Association
of Sex Educators, Counselors and Therapists of
Washington,
D.C., and is a Certified Sex Therapist. He holds a
certificate in Rational-Emotive Counseling from The
Institute for Advanced Study in Rational Psychotherapy,
chartered by the Regents of the University of the State
of New York.
Other works: GREEN IS THE GARDEN, a volume of
Poems; THE FACTS OF LIFE YOU ARE BEING
DENIED, non-fiction, a philosophical/psychological
approach to life. AN EPIC OF THE MIND. IF THE
HEAVEN BREAK OPEN. BEGGING THE
QUESTION. FLYING WITH SEAGULLS.